Melissa's
SOUTHERN
COOKBOOK

Melissa's
SOUTHERN
COOKBOOK

❖ TRIED-AND-TRUE FAMILY RECIPES ❖

Melissa Sperka

WITHDRAWN

THE COUNTRYMAN PRESS
A DIVISION OF W. W. NORTON & COMPANY
INDEPENDENT PUBLISHERS SINCE 1923

All photos by the author unless otherwise noted below:

Page 10: © edoneil/iStockphoto.com; 44: © wsmahar/iStockphoto.com;
66: © sanddebeautheil/Shutterstock.com; 68: © Lauri Patterson/iStockphoto.com;
94, 160, 168, 203: © Olha_Afanasieva/iStockphoto.com

For information about permission to reproduce selections from this book, write to Permissions,
The Countryman Press, 500 Fifth Avenue, New York, NY 10110

For information about special discounts for bulk purchases, please contact
W. W. Norton Special Sales at specialsales@wwnorton.com or 800-233-4830.

Manufacturing by Quad/Graphics, Taunton
Book design by Seton Rossini

The Countryman Press
www.countrymanpress.com

A division of W. W. Norton & Company, Inc.
500 Fifth Avenue, New York, NY 10110
www.wwnorton.com

978-1-58157-383-1

10 9 8 7 6 5 4 3 2 1

This cookbook is dedicated to my amazing sons, Chase and Jordan.
You are a dream come true and you both are destined for greatness.
I'll love you forever.

Contents

INTRODUCTION

The tradition of gathering around the kitchen table is a long-held practice for my entire family, dating back generations. My parents made daily mealtime a routine happening filled with lively conversation, and an opportunity to reconnect after a busy day. Empty chairs were often filled with friends and family who happened to stop by for a visit.

Likewise, there were never any empty chairs at either of my grandparents' kitchen tables. My grandparents lived on the food they grew and harvested on their Virginia farmland. In addition to the work at the home place, each grandfather also had a career apart from the responsibilities they handled at home. They were part of a generation whose roles were traditional, so my Southern grandmothers tended to the household. Part of that was overseeing the daily activities of the kids and preparing a plethora of homegrown dishes to feed a large family fit for a king. The days typically began with a hearty breakfast consisting of bacon and eggs, grits, biscuits smothered in sausage gravy, or buttermilk pancakes—or any combination of the aforementioned— along with plenty of strong black coffee. At the end of the day, the table might be filled with Southern-fried chicken or meat loaf, macaroni and cheese, green beans, mashed potatoes, and corn on the cob, with sliced tomatoes and cucumbers from the garden. A pan of hot buttered corn bread was sure to be nearby along with a gallon or two of sweet tea to wash it all down. Everyone was welcome at the supper table—family, neighbors, and friends alike.

I watched my own mother continue this tradition as her mother did before her, canning, freezing, and cooking the fresh produce that my dad grew and still grows in his backyard garden. This birthed in me a passion and love for cooking and baking and the Southern family traditions that were instilled in me from a very young age. It also ignited the desire to share that passion with others. In the pages of this book, I include many of my own family's favorite recipes as well as pay homage to those generations before me who inspired my love of cooking and baking. That same passion continues to inspire me every day to live my very best life, Southern style.

Starters: Dips, Munchables, & Beverages

In my love of entertaining through the years, I've discovered that the tone for most parties and casual get-togethers is set at the very beginning around the appetizer table. When people casually share a dish, it often results in friendly banter and conversation, establishing new relationships and friendships. I wouldn't dream of hosting guests in my home without at least one appetizer and a fun featured drink. When planning this part of the event, simplicity is key and you must consider your guests' needs in the process.

BLACK-EYED PEA HUMMUS

Hummus is a traditional Mediterranean dip made from ground chickpeas. To enhance the smooth and silky texture, it's typically made using a ground sesame seed butter called tahini paste. Tahini paste can be a bit pricey, so for this Southern spin-off, I chose to use peanut butter instead. Peanut butter lends a nutty flavor to the black-eyed pea purée without breaking the bank.

Yield: About 2 cups hummus

3 garlic cloves, peeled

2 (14-ounce) cans black-eyed peas, drained and rinsed

3 tablespoons freshly squeezed lemon juice

3 tablespoons olive oil, plus more for drizzling

2 tablespoons creamy peanut butter

1 teaspoon spicy sesame oil

1 teaspoon ground cumin

1 teaspoon salt

½ teaspoon smoked paprika

½ teaspoon ground ancho chili powder

¼ teaspoon freshly ground black pepper

4 dashes hot sauce

6 pita pockets, cut into triangles, for serving

Place the garlic in the bowl of a food processor. Process until finely minced.

Add the remaining ingredients, except pita pockets. Continue to pulse until smooth.

Cover and chill for 2 hours.

Serve drizzled with additional olive oil and pita triangles.

PERFECT GUACAMOLE

Mexican food is always a crowd favorite and no fiesta would be complete without homemade guacamole. After much experimentation, this party dip is now perfection. Since avocados oxidize quickly, keep in mind you should make this on the day you intend to eat it.

One useful trick is to mix a couple of the pits into the guacamole, which seems to have a magical effect on the oxidation process. When storing, press plastic wrap directly on the top, then cover tightly and keep chilled. The only thing left to do is grab a bag of tortilla chips and start scooping.

Yield: About 3 cups guacamole

5 medium-size avocados
¼ cup finely diced red onion
1 jalapeño pepper, finely diced
1 large Roma tomato, seeded and
    finely diced
2 garlic cloves, minced
2 tablespoons freshly squeezed lime
    juice
1 teaspoon salt
1 teaspoon ground cumin
1 teaspoon Mexican oregano
¼ teaspoon freshly ground black
    pepper

Peel and pit the avocados. Using a fork, mash the avocado flesh, leaving it chunky.

Add the remaining ingredients. Mix well.

Serve immediately or cover tightly and chill.

QUESO BLANCO DIP

This rich white cheese dip is the kind you might enjoy at your favorite Mexican restaurant. Made with white American cheese purchased from the deli at your local grocery store, it takes very few ingredients to make a batch at home and it works splendidly as a fiesta dip, drizzled on nachos, tacos, or burritos. It's sure to become a tailgating favorite with your family and friends.

Yield: About 4 cups dip

1½ pounds white American cheese, cubed

2 cups heavy cream

1 (4-ounce) can fire-roasted green chiles

In a heavy-bottomed saucepan, combine the American cheese and cream. Cook over medium heat, stirring, until the cheese has fully melted.

Add the green chiles. Mix well.

Serve immediately with tortilla chips or transfer to a slow cooker to keep warm.

HOMEMADE PIMIENTO CHEESE

Pimiento cheese is often referred to as "Southern pâté." That description works perfectly for me, although my love for pimiento cheese might tempt me to elevate it to the status of "Southern caviar." Slather it on bread, crackers, or celery ribs, or serve it as a dip with pretzels and corn chips—it's always the star of the show.

Yield: 4 cups pimiento cheese

2 cups real mayonnaise

4 ounces diced pimiento with juice

½ teaspoon Worcestershire sauce

½ teaspoon garlic salt

½ teaspoon onion powder

¼ teaspoon garlic powder

¼ teaspoon freshly ground black pepper

¼ teaspoon dry mustard

4 cups shredded sharp cheddar cheese

Whisk together the mayonnaise, pimiento, Worcestershire sauce, garlic salt, onion powder, garlic powder, black pepper, and mustard.

Mix in the cheddar cheese, stirring gently until the ingredients are evenly distributed. Chill for at least 2 hours before serving.

CAJUN CRAB DIP WITH GARLIC-HERB ROLL DIPPERS

You can't beat a fabulous dip that bakes the dippers along with it in the same skillet. I love placing this interactive dip in the center of the table, then stepping back and watching everyone dig in. There's never a scoop left over.

Yield: 16 servings

Rolls:

16 frozen yeast dinner rolls (see Cook's Note)

1 tablespoon unsalted butter, for pan

⅓ cup grated Parmesan cheese

1 tablespoon chopped fresh Italian parsley

1 teaspoon garlic salt

½ cup (1 stick, or 4 ounces) unsalted butter, melted

Dip:

4 ounces chive and onion cream cheese, softened

1 cup real mayonnaise

1 cup sour cream

2 tablespoons unsalted butter, melted

1½ tablespoons Cajun seasoning

1 teaspoon garlic powder

½ teaspoon seasoned salt

¼ teaspoon freshly ground black pepper

1 teaspoon hot sauce

2 cups shredded pepper Jack cheese, divided

8 ounces jumbo lump crabmeat

1 tablespoon chopped fresh chives

To make the rolls: Place the frozen dinner rolls on a waxed paper–lined baking sheet. Cover with plastic wrap. Allow to thaw at room temperature for 30 minutes. The dough should be thawed but still cold.

Butter the bottom and sides of a 12-inch cast-iron skillet.

Sift together the Parmesan cheese, parsley, and garlic salt into a 1-gallon resealable plastic bag.

Dip the thawed dinner rolls into the melted butter. Toss them in the plastic bag that contains the Parmesan cheese mixture. Arrange side by side around the edge of the prepared skillet. Cover with plastic wrap and let rise for 2 to 2½ hours, or until doubled.

To make the dip: Preheat the oven to 350°F.

In a medium-size mixing bowl, using an electric mixer on medium-high speed, whip together the cream cheese, mayonnaise, sour cream, melted butter, Cajun seasoning, garlic powder, seasoned salt, black pepper, and hot sauce until fully combined.

By hand, mix in 1 cup of the pepper Jack cheese, the crabmeat, and chives. Unwrap the skillet and pour the cheese mixture into the center of the skillet. Top with the remaining cup of shredded pepper Jack cheese.

Bake for 30 minutes, or until the rolls are golden and the dip is heated through, covering the rolls with aluminum foil during the final 10 minutes of baking to prevent overbrowning, if needed.

Let rest for 5 minutes on the counter before serving.

COOK'S NOTE:

The frozen yeast dinner rolls used in this recipe are *un*baked. They are small rounds of frozen dough that can be found in the frozen section of most grocery stores.

PUFF PASTRY-WRAPPED SMOKIES

Pigs in a blanket are consummate party food. It doesn't matter how fancy the gathering—they seem to always be one of the first appetizers to go. Serve these puff pastry-wrapped smokies with honey Dijon mustard and spicy ketchup on the side for dipping and watch 'em disappear.

Yield: 24 smokies

All-purpose flour, for dusting
½ (17.3-ounce) package puff pastry
    (1 sheet), thawed
1 large egg
1 tablespoon cold water
24 mini-beef smokies
Poppy seeds
Toasted sesame seeds
Honey Dijon mustard and spicy
    ketchup, for dipping

Preheat the oven to 400°F. Line a standard baking sheet with parchment paper.

On a lightly floured surface, roll out the puff pastry sheet to a roughly 14-inch square. Using a pizza cutter, cut into 24 equal squares.

In a small mixing bowl, whisk together the egg and cold water. Lightly brush onto the puff pastry squares.

Place a smokie on each square and roll, ending seam side down. Place at least 1 inch apart on the prepared baking sheet.

Brush the tops and sides of the pastry-wrapped smokies with the egg wash. Sprinkle one dozen of the pastries with poppy seeds and the other dozen with toasted sesame seeds.

Bake for 15 to 17 minutes, or until golden. Serve immediately with honey Dijon mustard and spicy ketchup, for dipping.

FRIED GREEN TOMATOES

Fried green tomatoes are a time-honored summer tradition in the South. They're made using unripened tomatoes that are breaded in cornmeal and then fried until crispy and golden. Contrary to popular thought, not all green tomatoes are equal, as each variety of tomato has a slightly different taste. Choose an unripened tomato that's firm when squeezed.

For the best results, the crispy cornmeal coating should be gently pressed onto the sliced tomatoes before gently lowering each piece into the oil for frying. They're a bona-fide indulgence and one we look forward to enjoying every year.

Yield: 10 to 12 slices tomato

2 large green tomatoes
1 cup all-purpose flour, divided
2 large eggs
2 tablespoons whole buttermilk
1 teaspoon hot sauce
¾ cup self-rising yellow cornmeal
1 teaspoon seasoned salt
½ teaspoon garlic powder
½ teaspoon onion powder
½ teaspoon paprika
½ teaspoon freshly ground black
    pepper
Vegetable oil, for frying

Slice the tomatoes into ¼-inch-thick slices. Lay the slices in a single layer on a paper towel. Gently press another paper towel on top. Let rest for 10 minutes.

To prepare the dredging station, place ½ cup of the flour on a plate. Whisk together the eggs, buttermilk, and hot sauce in a shallow dish or bowl. On a second plate, mix the remaining ½ cup of flour with the cornmeal, seasoned salt, garlic powder, onion powder, paprika, and pepper. Line up the dishes in that order.

In a large, heavy-bottomed skillet, heat about 1 inch of vegetable oil to 350° to 360°F. Line a baking sheet with paper towels and place near the stovetop.

Dredge the tomato slices first in the plain flour, then in the egg mixture, then in the seasoned cornmeal. Press the breading onto all sides of the tomato slices.

Working in batches to avoid overcrowding the pan, carefully lower the breaded slices into the hot oil. Cook for 4 to 5 minutes, gently turning as needed until golden.

Transfer the fried tomato slices from the oil with a slotted spoon to the lined baking sheet. Season with additional seasoned salt. Repeat until all the tomato slices are fried.

Serve immediately.

SWEET-AND-SOUR MEATBALLS

These scrumptious sweet-and-sour meatballs are a must-make for your next party. The hand-rolled meatballs can be prepared and cooked in advance and then chilled or frozen. To prepare for serving, whisk together the sauce, place the cooked meatballs into a slow cooker, then pour the sauce on top. Simmer on LOW for a couple of hours and voilà, they're ready to eat!

Yield: About 40 meatballs

Meatballs:

1 pound lean ground beef

1 pound ground pork

½ cup panko breadcrumbs

2 large eggs, beaten

½ cup whole milk

1 medium-size sweet onion, finely diced

2 tablespoons grated Parmesan cheese

1 tablespoon Worcestershire sauce

2 teaspoons garlic salt

1 teaspoon dried Italian seasoning or oregano

½ teaspoon freshly ground black pepper

Sauce:

12 ounces pineapple preserves

1 cup ketchup

½ cup sweet Asian chili sauce

3 tablespoons teriyaki sauce

3 tablespoons cider vinegar

Preheat the oven to 400°F. Use a broiler pan or a rimmed baking pan fitted with an oven-safe rack and spray with cooking spray. Set aside.

In a medium-size mixing bowl, mix together the beef, pork, breadcrumbs, eggs, milk, onion, Parmesan cheese, Worcestershire sauce, garlic salt, Italian seasoning, and pepper.

Roll into 1-inch balls and place 1 inch apart on the prepared baking pan. Bake for 20 to 22 minutes, or until no pink remains. Drain off any excess fat.

Meanwhile, to make the sauce: In a medium-size saucepan, mix together the pineapple preserves, ketchup, chili sauce, teriyaki sauce, and cider vinegar. Heat over medium heat until the preserves have completely melted.

If serving immediately, add the cooked meatballs to the saucepan and gently stir to coat with the sauce. Simmer gently for 20 to 30 minutes, then keep warm until serving.

To slow cook, place the cooked meatballs in a slow cooker and pour the warm sauce on top. Simmer on LOW for 2 hours, then keep warm until serving.

COOK'S NOTE:
If using frozen meatballs in a slow cooker, increase the cooking time to 4 hours on LOW, or until the meatballs are heated through.

ROAST BEEF CROSTINI WITH HORSERADISH MAYONNAISE, BLUE CHEESE, AND CHIVES

This elegant appetizer is a cinch to make. It's spectacular for serving as a hearty appetizer on Christmas, New Year's Eve, or any special occasion. The creamy horseradish mayonnaise and blue cheese crumbles make the perfect accompaniment to the tender, thinly sliced roast beef and, on the crispy garlic crostini, the flavors marry beautifully.

Yield: 16 crostini

1 (14-inch) French baguette, sliced
2 tablespoons olive oil
1 teaspoon garlic salt, divided
⅔ cup real mayonnaise
2 tablespoons heavy cream
1 tablespoon prepared horseradish
1 pound thinly sliced deli roast beef
2 ounces blue cheese crumbles
3 tablespoons chopped fresh chives

Preheat the oven to 400°F. Slice the baguette into 16 equal slices. Arrange on a baking sheet.

Mix the olive oil with ½ teaspoon of the garlic salt and lightly brush the baguette slices. Toast in the oven for 8 minutes, then let cool.

Whisk together the mayonnaise, cream, horseradish, and remaining ½ teaspoon of garlic salt.

Lightly spread each toasted baguette slice with the horseradish mayonnaise. Top with the roast beef.

Dollop a small amount of horseradish mayonnaise on top and sprinkle with crumbled blue cheese and chopped chives.

Arrange the assembled crostini on a platter and serve immediately.

SRIRACHA LIME SHRIMP COCKTAIL SHOOTERS

These shrimp cocktail shooters are a fantastic way to bring in the New Year. They're simple to make and easy to hold while talking around the appetizer table. Drape one cooked shrimp on the side of the shot glass for dipping and then serve the remaining shrimp on the side over ice for those who want to indulge a little more and not waste a drop of the kicked-up cocktail sauce.

Yield: 12 shooters plus 20 shrimp on the side

Shrimp:
64 ounces vegetable stock
2 lemons, quartered
4 garlic cloves, peeled
1 tablespoon kosher salt
2 teaspoons lemon pepper
32 large raw, tail-on shrimp, peeled and deveined

Cocktail Sauce:
12 ounces chili sauce
½ cup ketchup
1 tablespoon freshly squeezed lime juice
1 tablespoon sriracha
1 teaspoon wasabi paste (see Cook's Note)
1 teaspoon seafood seasoning
1 teaspoon onion powder
Fresh dill sprigs, for garnish

Place the vegetable stock into a large pot. Add the lemon quarters, garlic, salt, and lemon pepper. Bring to a boil, then lower the heat to medium and simmer for 10 minutes. Use a slotted spoon to remove the lemon quarters and garlic.

Have ready a bowl of ice water. Increase the heat to medium-high and drop the shrimp into the simmering stock. Cook for 2 to 3 minutes, or until pink and curled. Remove from the stock and drop into the ice water to immediately stop the cooking process.

Meanwhile, to make the cocktail sauce: Whisk together the chili sauce, ketchup, lime juice, sriracha, wasabi, seafood seasoning, and onion powder. Chill until ready to assemble the shooters.

To assemble, divide the cocktail sauce among 12 shooter glasses. Drape a cooked shrimp on the side of each glass and garnish with sprigs of fresh dill. Serve the remaining cooked shrimp on the side over ice.

Keep chilled or serve immediately.

COOK'S NOTE:
1 teaspoon prepared horseradish may be substituted for the wasabi paste.

EGG SALAD WITH ROASTED RED PEPPER AND OLIVES

Egg salad is one of those classic salads that are handy to have prepared and chilling in the refrigerator. It can be enjoyed with crackers or celery as a between-meal snack or slathered on bread and eaten as a sandwich on busy days when there's no time to cook. This version combines the subtle sweetness of roasted red pepper with the saltiness of pimiento-stuffed green olives—the two combine to knock the flavor of this easy egg salad out of the park.

Yield: About 3 cups egg salad

8 large hard-boiled eggs
⅔ cup real mayonnaise
1 tablespoon spicy brown mustard
2 teaspoons granulated sugar
2 teaspoons chopped fresh dill
1 teaspoon salt
½ teaspoon freshly ground
    black pepper
½ teaspoon garlic powder
½ teaspoon onion powder
¼ cup chopped dill pickles
¼ cup diced roasted red bell pepper
⅓ cup pimiento-stuffed green olives,
    halved

Peel and finely chop the hard-boiled eggs. Set aside.

In a medium-size mixing bowl, whisk together the mayonnaise, mustard, sugar, dill, salt, black pepper, garlic powder, and onion powder. Add the chopped egg, pickles, bell pepper, and green olives. Mix well.

Cover and chill for at least 3 hours before serving.

Serve with celery, crackers, or bread.

PULL-APART SUPREME PIZZA PINWHEELS

These pizza pinwheels are filled with the toppings you might enjoy on a loaded-up pie at your favorite pizza joint. Roll the filling in the dough, jelly roll–style, then slice and arrange on a pizza pan in a circle. Top with more cheese at the end of baking, then they're ready to serve with a side of warm pizza sauce for dipping. These pinwheels reign supreme as a twist on pizza for your game day munchies.

Yield: 16 servings

8 ounces sweet or spicy Italian sausage

½ cup diced onion

½ cup seeded and diced green bell pepper

4 ounces mushrooms, roughly chopped

½ teaspoon dried Italian seasoning

½ teaspoon garlic salt

½ teaspoon red pepper flakes

1 (13.8-ounce) can refrigerated classic pizza crust (e.g., Pillsbury), or homemade, such as ½ recipe No-Fail Pizza Dough (page 90)

1½ cups pizza sauce, divided

3 cups shredded mozzarella cheese, divided

¼ cup pitted and sliced black olives, patted dry

⅓ cup sliced mini pepperoni

1 tablespoon grated Parmesan cheese, plus more for serving (optional)

Preheat the oven to 375°F. Liberally spray a 16-inch pizza pan with cooking spray. Set aside.

In a medium-size skillet, heat a light drizzle of olive oil. Add the sausage, onion, green bell pepper, and mushrooms. Season with the Italian seasoning, garlic salt, and red pepper flakes. Cook for 10 minutes, or until no pink remains in the sausage. Remove from the heat and drain or spread onto double-lined paper towels to remove excess oil.

Stretch the pizza crust into a roughly 12 × 16-inch rectangle. Spread with ½ cup of the pizza sauce and sprinkle with 1 cup of the mozzarella cheese. Sprinkle the crumbled sausage mixture over the cheese, arranging the black olive and mini pepperoni slices on top. Cover with 1 cup of the mozzarella cheese.

Begin to roll, starting with the widest edge. Use a sharp knife to carefully cut into 16 equal portions. When cutting into portions, if the rolls come apart slightly, don't panic; rewrap and press together. Place side by side on the prepared pan, starting in the center of the pan and forming into a circle (see Cook's Note). As the cheese melts and the dough bakes, the filling will adhere.

Bake for 20 minutes, or until golden. Sprinkle with the Parmesan cheese and the remaining cup of mozzarella cheese. Continue to bake for another 5 minutes, or until the cheese melts.

Sprinkle with additional grated Parmesan cheese before serving, if desired, and serve with the remaining cup of warm pizza sauce on the side, for dipping.

COOK'S NOTE:
Alternatively, these pizza pinwheels may be baked individually in muffin cups.

PARMESAN CRUMB-TOPPED TOMATO SLAB PIE

This tomato slab pie is tasty enough to serve as an appetizer yet, elegant enough to serve as a light meal with a salad. Fresh tomato slices are topped with buttery Parmesan and panko crumb topping and it's then baked on a pizza crust until the crust and topping are crispy and golden. From start to finish, it comes together in under 30 minutes.

Yield: Serves 12 pieces

3 large tomatoes, sliced into 12 slices

1 teaspoon kosher salt

1 (13.8-ounce) can refrigerated classic pizza crust (e.g., Pillsbury), or homemade, such as ½ recipe No-Fail Pizza Dough (page 90)

8 ounces chive and onion cream cheese, softened

3 tablespoons real mayonnaise

1 teaspoon garlic salt

½ teaspoon onion powder

2 cups shredded mozzarella or Italian blend cheese, divided

1½ teaspoons dried Italian seasoning, divided

¼ cup panko breadcrumbs

2 tablespoons grated Parmesan cheese

2 tablespoons salted butter, melted

Preheat the oven to 425°F. Liberally spray a standard 17 × 12-inch rimmed baking sheet with cooking spray. Set aside.

Place the tomato slices in a single layer on paper towels. Sprinkle with the salt. Gently press another paper towel on top. Allow the tomato slices to release some of the juices while you prepare the rest of the ingredients.

Press the pizza dough evenly into the prepared pan. Set aside.

Use an electric mixer to whip together the cream cheese, mayonnaise, garlic salt, and onion powder. Spread evenly onto the dough. Sprinkle with 1 cup of the mozzarella cheese.

Arrange the tomato slices over the crust, then sprinkle with 1 teaspoon of the Italian seasoning and the remaining cup of mozzarella cheese.

In a small bowl, mix together the panko breadcrumbs, Parmesan cheese, melted butter, and remaining ½ teaspoon of Italian seasoning. Sprinkle over the top of the mozzarella cheese.

Bake for 15 to 18 minutes, or until the topping and the crust are golden. Cut into 12 pieces and serve.

RAINBOW SHERBET PARTY PUNCH

This colorful punch is so festive and fun to make. One sip and it's like being transported back to my childhood birthday parties. When making punch, keep in mind everything needs to be thoroughly chilled beforehand and assembled just before serving for the sweetest results. To expedite assembly, scoop the sherbet into balls in advance and place on a wax paper–lined baking sheet, then pop them back into the freezer until the party begins.

Yield: About 25 servings

64 ounces pineapple juice, chilled

24 ounces no-pulp orange juice, chilled

2 liters lemon-lime soda, chilled

2 quarts rainbow sherbet

Sprigs of fresh mint, for garnish (optional)

In a large punch bowl (see Cook's Note), mix together the chilled pineapple juice and orange juice.

Pour enough chilled lemon-lime soda into the bowl, leaving at least 4 inches at the top to allow for displacement.

Use a 4-ounce ice-cream scoop to scoop the rainbow sherbet on top.

Garnish with sprigs of fresh mint, if desired.

COOK'S NOTE:
The size of the punch bowl used could affect how much lemon-lime soda will be necessary. Adjust the amount accordingly, leaving enough headspace for the rainbow sherbet.

SPARKLING STRAWBERRY LEMONADE

Sultry Southern summers call for tall glasses of ice-cold drinks. When strawberries are in season, it would be a travesty not to enjoy at least one glass of strawberry lemonade to cool you down. Seltzer water adds a bit of sparkle and turns this thirst quencher into an occasion to invite over your neighbors to sit a spell and catch up. There's only one problem: They may never leave.

Yield: About ½ gallon lemonade, when combined with 1-liter seltzer water

2 cups water
2 cups granulated sugar
1 quart strawberries, hulled and cubed
2 cups freshly squeezed lemon juice
1 liter seltzer water, chilled
Lemon slices and whole strawberries, for garnish (optional)

Simmer the water and sugar together in a medium-size saucepan over medium-high heat on the stovetop. Stir until the sugar has completely dissolved, then set aside to cool.

Purée the strawberries in a food processor or stand blender. Push through a fine-mesh sieve or cheesecloth to remove the seeds and pulp.

Whisk together the sugar mixture, puréed strawberries, and lemon juice until fully blended. Chill thoroughly.

To serve, fill glasses two-thirds full with strawberry lemonade, then fill the rest of the way with chilled seltzer water just before serving.

Garnish with lemon slices and whole strawberries, if desired.

PINEAPPLE LEMONADE JULEPS

While watching the Kentucky Derby each year I like to have a family-friendly signature drink ready for all of us to enjoy. Once I featured this fruit juice–laced julep, the race for the best drink was over. It got rave reviews and has been regularly requested by friends and family ever since.

Yield: About 3 quarts julep

2 cups granulated sugar

2 cups water

2 cups pineapple juice

2 cups low-sugar apple juice

1¼ cups freshly squeezed lemon juice

1 liter seltzer water, chilled

Lemon slices

Fresh mint sprigs

In a medium-size saucepan over medium-high heat, bring the sugar and water to a simmer. Simmer for 5 minutes, or until the sugar crystals are completely dissolved. Remove from the heat and let cool completely.

In a one-gallon pitcher, mix the cooled sugar mixture together with the pineapple juice, apple juice, and lemon juice. Chill thoroughly.

Just before serving, add the chilled seltzer water. Stir well. Garnish with lemon slices and sprigs of fresh mint.

FRESH PEACH TEA

It's no secret we Southerners love sweet tea. This variation utilizes fresh peaches, giving it a spectacular twist on flavor. It's a satisfying way to quench your thirst on a sultry summer afternoon, and an opportunity to celebrate the favored summer fruit of the South.

Yield: 8 servings

4 large ripe peaches, divided
4 cups cold water, plus more for
    serving
4 family-size tea bags
1 cup granulated sugar
½ cup freshly squeezed lemon juice
Fresh mint sprigs

Halve two of the peaches, removing the pits. Cut into ½-inch slices. Place in a single layer on a parchment-lined baking sheet. Freeze for at least 4 hours until solid, or overnight.

In a medium-size saucepan, bring 4 cups of cold water to a rolling boil. Remove from the heat and add the tea bags. Cover and allow the tea to steep for 12 minutes.

Remove the tea bags and add the sugar, stirring until completely dissolved.

Peel, pit, and cube the remaining two peaches. Purée with the lemon juice in a food processor or stand blender. Push through a fine-mesh strainer to remove the pulp.

Pour the peach purée into a 2½-quart pitcher along with the sweetened tea. Fill to three-quarters full with additional cold water. Stir well and chill.

Serve in decorative glasses, using the frozen peach slices in place of ice cubes. Garnish with mint.

Breakfast Bounty

Breakfast in the South truly is the most important meal of the day. In light of our love of breakfast fare, "breakfast for supper" is equally as popular. In the old days, a traditional big, hearty breakfast was necessary for the long hours of hard manual labor that were sure to follow. These days, we still love our traditional breakfast offerings, such as biscuits, sausage gravy, buttery grits, and hash browns, but we've definitely expanded our menus to include other dishes—such as quiche, breakfast casseroles, cheesy omelets, sweet rolls, and croissants, as well as cinnamon- and fruit-laced quick breads, to name a few. There's always room for more dishes to love at the family breakfast table.

SAUSAGE GRAVY AND CREAM BISCUITS

Hot biscuits smothered in sausage gravy are a breakfast tradition in the South. While the ingredients are simple, the techniques sometimes vary from one cook to another. Start any day with this down-home, stick-to-your-ribs kind of food that won't break the bank.

Yield: 6 servings (2 biscuits per person)

Cream Biscuits:

3 cups self-rising flour, plus more for dusting

2 cups heavy cream

3 tablespoons salted butter, melted

Sausage Gravy:

1 pound mild country sausage

½ cup all-purpose flour

1 teaspoon plain or seasoned salt

1 teaspoon freshly ground black pepper

5 cups whole milk

To make the biscuits: Preheat the oven to 425°F and line two baking sheets with parchment paper. Set aside.

Place the self-rising flour in a medium-size mixing bowl. Make a well in the center and pour the cream into it.

Using a fork, work the flour into the cream just until moistened. Turn out the dough onto a lightly floured, nonstick surface and gently turn two or three times to coat.

Use a floured rolling pin to roll the biscuit dough about ¾ inch thick. Cut into rounds using a 3-inch biscuit cutter. Place 2 inches apart on the prepared pan.

Brush the tops of the biscuits with the melted butter. Bake for 10 to 12 minutes.

After baking, brush the tops with additional melted butter and change the oven setting to BROIL for 2 to 3 additional minutes to brown the tops.

To make the sausage gravy: While the biscuits are baking, brown the sausage in a large skillet over medium-high heat. Cook until no pink remains. Drain all but 3 tablespoons of fat from the skillet.

Sprinkle the sausage with the all-purpose flour, salt, and pepper. Cook over medium heat, stirring, until the flour is fully moistened and light beige in color and the sausage is coated.

Increase the heat to medium-high and add the milk, stirring constantly. Bring to a simmer to thicken, then lower the heat, allowing the gravy to gently bubble for 5 minutes. Taste and adjust the salt and pepper to taste, adding additional milk, if needed, to thin.

After the gravy has thickened, serve immediately, drizzled over the hot biscuits.

MAPLE SAUSAGE CROISSANT BREAKFAST BAKE

I can't think of anything that goes better with sausage than French toast or pancakes with plenty of pure maple syrup. This overnight casserole turns mini croissants into a cross between the two. The sausage links and croissants are soaked overnight in a creamy maple syrup–laced egg custard. In the morning, uncover and bake until puffy and golden. Add a sprinkle of powdered sugar and a drizzle of maple syrup and you'll think you're dining al fresco in a French bistro instead of at your own kitchen table at home.

Yield: 12 servings

16 fully cooked breakfast sausage links
16 baked mini croissants
6 large eggs
1 cup heavy cream
½ cup whole milk
⅓ cup pure maple syrup
¼ cup granulated sugar
¼ teaspoon salt
Powdered sugar and pure maple
    syrup, for serving

Spray an 8 × 12-inch shallow casserole dish with cooking spray. Set aside.

Cut the sausage links into thirds and the mini croissants into fourths. Arrange in the prepared baking dish.

In a small mixing bowl with a spout, whisk together the eggs, cream, milk, maple syrup, granulated sugar, and salt. Pour evenly over the croissants and sausages. Cover tightly with plastic wrap and refrigerate overnight.

To bake, preheat the oven to 325°F. Remove the plastic wrap. Bake for 45 to 50 minutes, or until puffy and golden.

Serve immediately, dusted with powdered sugar and a drizzle of maple syrup.

BACON AND EGG HASH BROWN NESTS

I knew I was onto a good thing when *Southern Living Magazine* wanted to include my Nested Potato Skins recipe in its September 2012 issue. Since then, I've filled these famous little hash brown potato nests with a plethora of different ingredients to suit the occasion. This bacon and egg variation can be served for breakfast or brunch and has the bonus of portion control, too.

Yield: 12 servings

1 (20-ounce) package refrigerated shredded hash browns

1 cup shredded Colby-Jack cheese

½ cup shredded Parmesan cheese

1 teaspoon garlic salt

½ teaspoon freshly ground black or white pepper

12 medium eggs (see Cook's Note)

Salt and freshly ground black pepper

4 strips bacon, cooked and crumbled

1 tablespoon chopped fresh chives

Preheat the oven to 450°F. *Liberally* spray the cups of a standard 12-cup nonstick muffin tin with cooking spray. Set aside.

In a medium-size mixing bowl, stir together the hash browns, Colby-Jack cheese, Parmesan cheese, garlic salt, and pepper. Mix until the ingredients are evenly distributed. Divide evenly among the 12 prepared muffin cups. Press firmly onto the bottom and sides of the cups.

Place in the oven and bake for 20 minutes, or until lightly golden. Lower the oven temperature to 425°F. Remove the muffin tin from the oven and quickly crack one egg into each nest. Season the eggs with salt and black pepper and return to the oven for 12 to 15 minutes, or until the eggs are cooked to your preference.

Gently loosen the edges of the nests with a knife and let rest for 5 minutes before attempting to remove from the pan.

Carefully transfer the nests to a plate or platter. Sprinkle with the crumbled bacon and chopped chives.

COOK'S NOTE:
Do not use larger eggs, which might overfill the hash browns.

HAM AND SWISS OMELET CUPS

Ham and eggs go together like peas and carrots. These muffin cups are fun to make and are terrific for making single-size servings, as well. Enjoy them on their own, on a hot homemade buttermilk biscuit, or on a toasted English muffin for a tasty breakfast on the run.

Yield: 8 omelet cups

8 slices smoked deli ham

6 large eggs

2 tablespoons sour cream

¼ teaspoon salt

¼ teaspoon freshly ground black
    pepper

¼ teaspoon dry mustard

2 green onions, finely chopped,
    divided

1 cup shredded Swiss cheese, divided

Preheat the oven to 375°F. Spray eight cups of a standard-size 12-cup muffin tin with cooking spray. Fit one slice of ham into each of the prepared cups. Set aside.

In a small mixing bowl, whisk together the eggs, sour cream, and seasonings. Add half of the green onions to the beaten eggs.

Distribute half of the Swiss cheese among each of the prepared muffin cups, then fill each cup three-quarters full with the beaten egg mixture. Sprinkle each with the remaining Swiss cheese.

Bake for 15 to 17 minutes, or until puffy and the centers are set when the pan is gently shaken.

Garnish with the remaining green onions and serve.

SPINACH AND BACON CHEDDAR QUICHE

I'm here to dispel the myth that real men don't eat quiche. All of the men in my family love this bacon-laced quiche and don't seem to mind the spinach. That makes this recipe a total score for Mom getting the boys to eat more vegetables. When making this savory pie, you may use a homemade piecrust or a quality frozen deep-dish crust. Either way this quiche is guaranteed to charm even the most reluctant quiche eaters.

Yield: Serves 8

1 (9-inch) frozen deep-dish piecrust, or homemade, such as ½ recipe Easy Piecrust (page 176)

1½ cups shredded sharp cheddar cheese, divided

1 cup packed baby spinach, roughly chopped

½ pound bacon, cooked and crumbled

6 large eggs

1 cup heavy cream

1 teaspoon garlic salt

½ teaspoon freshly ground black pepper

½ teaspoon onion powder

⅛ teaspoon ground nutmeg

Preheat the oven to 375°F. Remove the piecrust from the packaging and prick the bottom with a fork. Place on a baking sheet and into the oven to parbake for 5 minutes.

Divide the cheddar cheese into thirds and the spinach and bacon in half. Layer the cheese, spinach, and bacon into the parbaked crust twice in that order, reserving the final ½ cup of cheese for the top.

Whisk together the eggs, cream, and seasonings. Pour evenly over the layers and top with the remaining ½ cup of cheese. Shake gently to settle the custard into the layered ingredients.

Bake at 375°F for 10 minutes, and then lower the oven temperature to 350°F. Continue to bake for an additional 30 to 40 minutes, or until the center is set when gently shaken.

Remove from the oven and let rest on the counter for at least 20 minutes prior to cutting and serving.

COUNTRY SAUSAGE AND GRITS CASSEROLE

This recipe features one of the favorite foods of the South. Grits are inexpensive and can be prepared in a variety of different ways, depending on the meal. This hearty casserole is a fabulous way to include grits and sausage together on the breakfast menu. It's a must-make dish for a special holiday breakfast or brunch.

Yield: 12 servings

1 pound ground breakfast pork
　　sausage
1 small red bell pepper, seeded and
　　diced
4 green onions, thinly sliced
Salt and freshly ground black pepper

Grits
3 cups low-sodium chicken stock, plus
　　more as needed
3 cups whole milk
6 tablespoons salted butter, divided
1 tablespoon garlic salt
2 cups quick-cooking grits
3 ounces cream cheese, softened
3 cups shredded pepper Jack cheese,
　　divided

Preheat the oven to 350°F. Spray an 8 × 12-inch baking dish with cooking spray. Set aside.

In a medium-size skillet, heat a couple of drizzles of olive oil over medium-high heat. Cook the sausage, bell pepper, and green onions until no pink remains in the sausage and the vegetables have softened. Season lightly with salt and black pepper to taste. Drain all excess fat from the pan. Set aside.

To make the grits: In a heavy-bottomed saucepan, bring the chicken stock, milk, 4 tablespoons of the butter and the garlic salt to a boil.

Whisking constantly, gradually add the grits. Lower the temperature to low, cover, and simmer, stirring periodically to prevent sticking and adding additional chicken stock as needed to thin, for 20 minutes, or until all of the liquid has been absorbed and the grits have softened.

At the end of cooking, add the cream cheese. Stir until the cream cheese has completely melted.

Remove from the heat and mix in 1 cup of the pepper Jack cheese by hand.

Pour half of the cooked grits into the prepared casserole dish and spread evenly. Arranged the cooked sausage and vegetables on top. Sprinkle with 1 cup of the pepper Jack cheese.

Pour the remaining grits evenly over the sausage and top with the remaining cup of pepper Jack cheese. Dot with the remaining 2 tablespoons of butter.

Bake for 35 to 40 minutes, or until golden and bubbly. Remove from the oven, let rest for 10 minutes, and then serve.

ALMOST FAMOUS CINNAMON ROLLS

There are few things more comforting than the smell of cinnamon, sugar, and homemade bread wafting through the house. These cinnamon rolls are a cinch to make, thanks to rapid-rise yeast, and taste very much like a popular cinnamon roll at your local mall. Once perfected at home though, there's no need to stretch your budget again.

Yield: 24 cinnamon rolls

Dough:

2 (¼-ounce) packages rapid-rise dry yeast
½ cup warm water (110°–115°F)
1½ cups whole milk
½ cup granulated sugar
4 tablespoons salted butter, cubed
2 teaspoons salt
1 large egg, lightly beaten
5½ to 6 cups bread flour, plus more for kneading by hand (optional)

Filling:

½ cup (1 stick, or 4 ounces) salted butter, at room temperature, divided
½ cup granulated sugar
½ cup light brown sugar
¼ cup ground cinnamon
¼ teaspoon ground nutmeg

Frosting:

8 ounces cream cheese, softened
4 tablespoons salted butter, at room temperature
2 teaspoons pure vanilla extract
1 (16-ounce) box powdered sugar

To make the dough: In the bowl of a stand mixer fitted with a dough hook, dissolve the yeast in the warm water. Allow the yeast to bloom for 5 minutes.

In a small saucepan, combine the milk, granulated sugar, butter, and salt. Heat to between 110° and 115°F, stirring, until the butter has melted. *Do not boil.*

Add the warm milk mixture to the yeast in the mixing bowl. With the mixer running, mix in the egg.

Begin to add the bread flour, starting with 3 cups. Mix on low speed, stopping to scrape the sides of the bowl as needed.

Add 2 additional cups of bread flour. If the dough is still sticky, add more bread flour 1 tablespoon at a time, up to 6 cups total, until the dough leaves the sides of the bowl.

Increase the speed of the mixer and knead for 5 minutes. Alternatively, turn onto a floured surface and knead by hand for 5 minutes.

Coat the sides of a large bowl with cooking spray. Shape the dough into a ball and place in the bowl. Cover and place in a warm, draft-free place to rise for 1½ hours, or until doubled.

To fill the dough: Punch down the risen dough and stretch into a roughly 16 × 24-inch rectangle. Spread from end to end with 7 tablespoons of the butter, reserving the last tablespoon to butter a jelly-roll pan.

Mix together the granulated sugar, brown sugar, cinnamon, and nutmeg. Sprinkle over the buttered dough.

continued on next page

Begin rolling up the dough from the widest edge, ending seam side down.

Cut into 24 (1-inch) pieces and place side by side in a buttered jelly-roll pan. Cover and let rise for 1 hour, or until doubled.

Preheat the oven to 375°F. Uncover the dough and place the pan in the oven. Bake for 20 to 25 minutes, or until rolls are golden. Remove from the oven and let the rolls rest while you prepare the frosting.

To make the frosting: Cream together the cream cheese, butter, and vanilla. Gradually add the powdered sugar, beating until smooth. Spread evenly on top of the cinnamon rolls while hot.

Serve warm.

COOK'S NOTES:
These cinnamon rolls may be made the night before: After cutting into 24 (1-inch) portions, arrange in the buttered pan, cover, and then chill overnight. The dough will continue to rise very slowly in the refrigerator. Allow to rest at room temperature for *at least* 30 minutes to 1 hour, then bake accordingly.

DIJON SAUSAGE-STUFFED BISCUITS

I first enjoyed a simpler version of these sausage-stuffed biscuits at a brunch at our church. The recipe was so very basic that it was shared with me verbally on the spot. Being a fan of the combination of mustard and sausage, I began to rework the original recipe, experimenting with different seasonings and flavor combinations. These simple pastries were the result and the only thing left to talk about are the crumbs that remain on the platter.

Yield: 16 stuffed biscuits

1 pound breakfast pork sausage

8 ounces cream cheese, softened

2 green onions, finely chopped

3 tablespoons Dijon mustard, plus
    more for serving (optional)

½ teaspoon garlic salt

½ teaspoon freshly ground black
    pepper

1 (14-ounce) can big flaky biscuits
    (8-count)

1 large egg beaten with 1 tablespoon
    water

Preheat the oven to 350°F. Line a standard-size baking sheet with parchment paper. Set aside.

In a medium-size skillet over medium-high heat, sauté the sausage in a light drizzle of vegetable oil until no pink remains. Drain any excess fat from the pan. Lower the heat to medium-low.

Add the cream cheese, green onions, Dijon mustard, garlic salt, and pepper. Cook over low heat just until the cream cheese melts.

Remove the biscuit rounds from the can and cut in half through the middle, making 16 rounds total. Flatten each piece into a 3-inch circle.

Using a tablespoon, drop the sausage mixture into the center of each round. Brush the edges with the egg wash, then fold over the filling to form a half-moon. Seal the edges with a fork or a pastry wheel.

Place on the prepared baking sheet. Brush the top and sides of each biscuit with the remaining egg wash.

Bake for 14 to 15 minutes, or until golden, then serve with additional Dijon mustard for dipping, if desired.

CARAMEL APPLE CINNAMON FRENCH TOAST

This luscious overnight French toast is often thought of as a restaurant indulgence. It's so simple to make there's no reason you can't prepare this at home, too. The French toast is prepared in advance, then baked until it's puffy and beautifully golden. It's then topped with buttery sweet caramelized apples just before serving. This mouthwatering brunch dish falls into the category of restaurant quality in the comfort of your own home.

Yield: 8 servings

Overnight French Toast:

8 (1-inch-thick) slices French bread

1 cup heavy cream

½ cup granulated sugar

4 large eggs

2 teaspoons ground cinnamon

2 teaspoons pure vanilla extract

¼ teaspoon salt

Caramel Apples:

4 tablespoons salted butter

5 large Gala apples, peeled, cored, and sliced

1 teaspoon apple pie spice (see page 215 for a DIY substitution) or ground cinnamon

½ cup packed light brown sugar

1 teaspoon freshly squeezed lemon juice

2 tablespoons cornstarch, plus more if needed

¼ cup cold water, plus more if needed

1 teaspoon pure vanilla extract

To prepare the French toast: Butter a nonstick metal 9 × 13-inch baking pan.

Arrange the French bread slices in a single layer in the prepared pan.

In a small mixing bowl, whisk together the cream, granulated sugar, eggs, cinnamon, vanilla, and salt.

Pour evenly over the bread slices. Allow to sit for 10 minutes, then turn the bread. Cover with plastic wrap and refrigerate overnight.

The next day, preheat the oven to 425°F. Remove the plastic wrap from the French toast and bake for 25 minutes, or until golden and puffy, turning halfway through baking to brown both sides evenly, if desired.

To prepare the caramel apples: While the French toast is baking, melt the butter in a large skillet over medium-high heat. Add the sliced apples, apple pie spice, brown sugar, and lemon juice.

Bring to a simmer and then lower the heat. Cook over medium-low heat for 15 minutes, or until the apples are fork-tender.

To thicken the caramel sauce, dissolve the cornstarch in the cold water. Increase the heat to medium-high and mix in the cornstarch slurry, cooking for 1 to 2 minutes, or until thickened. Repeat if needed until the desired consistency is reached.

Remove from the heat and add the vanilla. Mix well. Serve immediately over the French toast or cover and chill if making in advance. Reheat before serving.

FRIED APPLES

Fried apples are scrumptious served as a side dish with ham or pork chops. They also work perfectly as a topping for hot buttered biscuits and buttermilk pancakes. They're especially tasty when apples are at their peak in season and the cool autumn breeze begins to blow.

Yield: About 4 cups apples

4 tablespoons salted butter
8 large Granny Smith apples, peeled cored and sliced
⅓ cup granulated sugar
⅓ cup light brown sugar
1 tablespoon freshly squeezed lemon juice
2 teaspoons ground cinnamon
1 teaspoon apple pie spice (see page 215 for a DIY substitution)
Pinch of salt
1 tablespoon cornstarch, plus more if needed
Cold water, as needed

In a heavy-bottomed skillet, melt the butter over medium-high heat.

Add the sliced apples, granulated sugar, brown sugar, lemon juice, cinnamon, apple pie spice, and salt. Mix until the ingredients are evenly distributed.

Lower the heat to low and simmer and bubble gently for 15 to 20 minutes to allow the sauce to thicken and reduce and until the apples slices are fork-tender.

To thicken the sauce, mix 1 tablespoon of cornstarch in just enough cold water to dissolve. Increase the heat and stir the cornstarch slurry into the apples. Repeat until the desired consistency is reached.

Serve immediately.

STRAWBERRY FREEZER JAM

Freezer jam is so simple to make, and when strawberries are in season, the possibilities in flavor combinations are endless. The addition of lemon and pineapple juice gives a subtle contrast to the sweetness of the berries and lends brightness to the flavor. The ease of preparation and the flavors combine to make this jam truly special for topping biscuits, toast, or scones.

Yield: 4 pints jam

2 quarts ripe, firm strawberries, hulled and cubed

2 tablespoons freshly squeezed lemon juice

4 cups fine granulated sugar

¾ cup pineapple juice

⅓ cup classic pectin

In a medium-size mixing bowl, use a potato masher to crush the strawberries, leaving them chunky.

Add the lemon juice and sugar. Mix well, then let stand for 10 minutes.

In a small saucepan, bring the pineapple juice and pectin to a boil, stirring constantly. Boil for 1 minute, or until the pectin has fully dissolved.

Add to the strawberries. Stir for 3 minutes, or until the sugar has fully dissolved.

Immediately pour into freezer-safe containers. Wipe the rims clean and fit each lid tightly on top. Leave at least ½ inch of headspace to allow for expansion.

Allow to sit on the counter for 24 hours to thicken, then freeze.

This jam will keep in the refrigerator for immediate use for up to 3 weeks or may be stored frozen for up to 1 year.

Thou Shalt Eat Bread

Here in the South, we have two notable house breads: buttermilk biscuits and corn bread. All Southern cooks have their own special recipe and techniques for making both kinds and may even boast that they can make the lightest, fluffiest biscuits around. Often these recipe "secrets" are handed down from previous generations.

Likewise, corn bread has many variations. The subject of savory versus sweet corn bread often ends in spirited debate where the two sides shall never meet and each remain adamant about its point of view. One or the other claims to know how "real" Southern corn bread should taste. Personally, I love a slightly sweet corn bread and am here to boldly say that, sweet or savory, it's *all* "real" Southern corn bread. There's no wrong way to prepare it as long as those eating it are satisfied.

When it comes to homemade bread making in any shape or form, it takes practice and even sometimes failure, but it can be mastered. Once you get the hang of it, I'm sure you'll agree that the smell of homemade bread baking is well worth the effort and the extra pounds that are sure to follow.

CLASSIC BUTTERMILK BISCUITS

The classic buttermilk biscuit needs no introduction. Every cook in the South claims to know the secret for making them perfect every time. Biscuit recipes are often handed down for generations, each featuring a twist that makes the recipe extra special. Perhaps it's a special way of folding the dough, or freezing the butter and then grating it instead of cutting it into the flour, or the amount of buttermilk used. The difference may be solely attributed to a local flour company that has the best biscuit-making flour around.

The truth of the matter is, biscuit making takes practice but there's no reason to shy away from making them yourself. Start with quality ingredients, and most important, remember not to overwork the dough. Biscuits should be tender and flaky and may be served at any meal but are enjoyed most often at breakfast. Homemade biscuits can be topped with a fresh slice of tomato from the garden, stacked with smoked Virginia ham, or smothered with rich country sausage gravy. It doesn't matter how you choose to serve them—buttermilk biscuits remain the favored house bread of the South.

Yield: 12 biscuits

3 cups self-rising flour
½ cup (1 stick, or 4 ounces) cold salted
    butter or shortening, cubed,
      plus 2 tablespoons melted, for
      brushing
1 cup whole buttermilk

Preheat the oven to 425°F. Butter the bottom and sides of a 10-inch cast-iron skillet (see Cook's Note). Set aside.

Place the flour and cubed butter in a medium-size mixing bowl. Using a pastry blender or two knives, cut the butter into the flour until it resembles coarse crumbs.

Make a well in the center and add the buttermilk. Using a fork, gradually work the flour into the buttermilk just until all the crumbs are moistened.

Turn out the dough onto a floured surface and gently turn two or three times, until the dough comes together and is no longer sticky. *Do not overflour.*

Roll out to a roughly ¾-inch thickness. Using a 2½-inch round biscuit cutter, cut into rounds. Place side by side in the prepared skillet.

Brush the tops with half of the melted butter. Bake for 18 to 20 minutes, or until puffy and golden.

Change the oven setting to BROIL. Broil for another 2 to 3 minutes to brown the biscuit tops.

Brush with the remaining melted butter and serve.

COOK'S NOTE:
You may bake these biscuits on a parchment-lined baking sheet, if desired.

FARMHOUSE SANDWICH BREAD

It would be difficult to top the aroma of freshly baked bread. When you take the time and effort to make it yourself, the love you put into it makes it taste even better. This farmhouse-style white bread makes the tastiest sandwich, French toast, and grilled cheese you'll ever eat in the comfort of your own kitchen. It's well worth the effort.

Yield: 2 loaves

2 (¼ ounce) packages rapid-rise dry
    yeast
½ cup warm water [110°–115°F]
1 cup whole milk
½ cup (1 stick, 4 ounces) unsalted
    butter, plus more for bowl
½ cup granulated sugar
2 teaspoons salt
1 large egg, beaten
4½ to 5 cups bread flour, plus more
    for dusting

In the bowl of a stand mixer, dissolve both packages of yeast with the warm water.

In a small saucepan, heat together the milk, butter, sugar, and salt to 110° to 115°F.

Add the warmed milk mixture to the yeast. Mix lightly to blend, then add the egg.

With the mixer running on low speed, begin to add the flour. Add the flour gradually until a soft dough forms.

Turn onto a floured surface and knead by hand four or five times, or until the dough is no longer sticky. Place in a large, buttered bowl and cover. Allow to rise in a draft-free place for 1½ hours, or until doubled.

Punch down the dough to release the air bubbles. Divide in half.

Butter two 9 × 5-inch loaf pans. Shape the divided dough into two loaves and place in the loaf pans. Cover and allow to rise for 30 minutes to 1 hour, or until doubled.

Preheat the oven to 375°F. Bake for 20 to 25 minutes, or until golden and the bread sounds hollow when tapped in the center. Let cool on a cooling rack.

Store tightly wrapped at room temperature. Eat within 2 days.

CHOCOLATE CHIP PEANUT BUTTER BANANA BREAD

Don't throw away over-ripe bananas—turn them into this moist bread loaded with chocolate chips. It's a fantastic twist on classic banana bread and will make adoring fans of the combination of peanut butter and chocolate extremely happy. Serve one loaf warm with a cup of coffee or hot tea and share the other with a friend.

Yield: 2 loaves

3 cups all-purpose flour, plus more for pans (optional)

1 teaspoon baking powder

½ teaspoon baking soda

1 teaspoon salt

⅔ cup smooth peanut butter

½ cup (1 stick, 4 ounces) unsalted butter, at room temperature, plus more for pans (optional)

2 teaspoons pure vanilla extract

¾ cup granulated sugar

¾ cup light brown sugar

3 large eggs

½ cup whole buttermilk

4 small ripe bananas, mashed (about 1½ cups)

1 cup semisweet chocolate chips

Preheat the oven to 350°F. Spray the bottom and sides of two standard 8 × 4-inch nonstick loaf pans with cooking spray or butter and flour. Set aside.

Sift together the all-purpose flour, baking powder, baking soda, and salt. Set aside.

In the bowl of a stand mixer, cream together the peanut butter, butter, and vanilla. Add the granulated sugar and brown sugar and beat for 2 minutes, or until creamy.

Add the eggs, one at a time, mixing well after each addition.

Reduce the speed of the mixer and add the sifted dry ingredients alternately with the buttermilk. After all has been added, beat just until fully combined, stopping to scrape the bottom and sides of the bowl periodically.

Fold in the mashed banana and chocolate chips by hand.

Divide the batter between the prepared loaf pans. Bounce the pans on the counter a few times to settle the batter and release any trapped air bubbles.

Bake, covering with foil midway through baking, if needed, to prevent overbrowning, for 40 to 45 minutes, or until a toothpick inserted into the center shows moist crumbs.

Let cool in the pan for 30 minutes, then carefully remove and place on a cooling rack to cool completely.

CINNAMON ROLL BREAD

This delicious quick bread is swirled with cinnamon and topped with a heavenly cream glaze. The sweet buttermilk dough can hardly contain the buttery brown sugar filling hiding within. There's no yeast, so no rising time is needed, which makes the preparation time quick and breezy.

Yield: 1 loaf

Dough:

2 cups all-purpose flour

1 cup granulated sugar

1 teaspoon baking powder

1 teaspoon salt

½ teaspoon baking soda

1 cup whole buttermilk

½ cup (1 stick, or 4 ounces) salted butter, melted and cooled

2 large eggs

2 teaspoons pure vanilla extract

Cinnamon Swirl:

4 tablespoons salted butter, melted

¼ cup light brown sugar

1 tablespoon ground cinnamon

Glaze:

1 cup powdered sugar

3 tablespoons heavy cream, plus more as needed, to thin

To make the dough: Preheat the oven to 350°F. Spray a 9 × 5-inch nonstick metal loaf pan with cooking spray. Set aside.

In a medium-size mixing bowl, sift together the flour, sugar, baking powder, salt, and baking soda.

In a separate bowl, whisk together the buttermilk, melted butter, eggs, and vanilla.

Add the wet to the dry ingredients, mixing until fully combined.

To make the cinnamon swirl: Mix together the melted butter, brown sugar, and ground cinnamon.

Pour half of the batter into the prepared loaf pan. Using a tablespoon, dollop half of the cinnamon swirl mixture over the top. Use a knife to swirl it through the batter.

Pour the remaining batter and cinnamon swirl on top, then repeat swirling the cinnamon through the batter with a knife.

Place in the oven and bake for 40 minutes. Check the center with a toothpick for doneness. If the center isn't cooked through, cover loosely with a piece of aluminum foil and continue to bake for an additional 10 to 15 minutes, or until a toothpick inserted into the center comes back clean.

Let cool on a cooling rack in the pan for 1 hour, then remove from the pan to cool completely.

To make the glaze: Mix the powdered sugar with the cream. Add more cream 1 tablespoon at a time until it reaches a spreading consistency. Pour over the cooled cinnamon roll bread.

EASY YEAST ROLLS

I can't think of a single occasion that fresh bread wouldn't be in order.
These yeast rolls use fast-acting yeast, which makes them light and fluffy, and they
come together in no time. Serve them fresh and hot right out of the oven with a
side of sweet cream butter. It doesn't get any better than that.

Yield: 30 rolls

5 cups bread flour
½ cup granulated sugar
2 (¼-ounce) packages rapid-rise dry
    yeast
1 tablespoon salt
1 large egg
½ cup (1 stick, or 4 ounces) plus
    2 tablespoons salted butter,
    divided, plus more for baking dish
1½ cups whole milk

In the bowl of a stand mixer fitted with a dough hook, blend together the flour, sugar, yeast, and salt.

Add the egg, mixing it into the dry ingredients.

In a small saucepan, melt the ½ cup of butter. Add the milk and heat until warm (110° to 115°F) but *do not boil.*

With the mixer on low speed, gradually add the warmed milk mixture. Continue until all the liquid has been added. Knead for 5 minutes.

Coat the inside of a mixing bowl generously with cooking spray. Form the dough into a round ball. Turn the dough to coat with the cooking spray. Cover and allow to rise for 1½ hours, or until doubled.

Punch down the dough. Pinch off 30 equal-size pieces. Roll the dough in your hands to form 2-inch balls. Place side by side in a buttered 9 × 13-inch baking dish or pan. Cover and allow to rise until doubled, about 1 hour.

Preheat the oven to 375°F. Bake for 25 to 30 minutes, or until golden. Brush the tops of the rolls with the remaining 2 tablespoons of melted butter while hot and just before serving.

FRENCH ONION SOUR CREAM BISCUITS

These biscuits are light and mildly fragrant with the addition of chives and garlic. The French onion dip gives savory subtle undertones to the dough, making it perfect to serve with a pot roast, meat loaf, or steak as dinner bread.

Yield: 10 biscuits

2 cups self-rising flour, plus more for dusting

2 teaspoons chopped fresh chives

½ teaspoon garlic powder

1 cup French onion dip

½ cup heavy cream, divided

2 tablespoons salted butter, melted

Preheat the oven to 450°F and line two standard baking sheets with parchment paper. Set aside.

Sift together the flour, chives and garlic powder.

Make a well in the center and add the French onion dip and ¼ cup of the cream.

Use a fork to gradually incorporate the flour, adding up to ¼ cup of additional cream until the flour is fully moistened.

Turn out the dough onto a floured nonstick surface and gently knead four times, coating lightly with flour on all sides.

Roll the dough to ¾-inch thickness. Use a 2½-inch biscuit cutter to cut into rounds. Reroll the scrap pieces as needed.

Place 1½ inches apart on the prepared baking sheets. Brush the tops with melted butter.

Bake for 10 minutes. Brush the tops with additional melted butter and broil for 2 minutes, until the tops are golden. Serve immediately.

GARLIC CHEDDAR BUTTERMILK BISCUITS

These cheesy biscuits are similar to the ones you may enjoy at a famous seafood restaurant. They're fluffy on the inside and filled with the flavor of garlic and freshly grated sharp cheddar cheese. I recommend that you bake them side by side in a cast-iron skillet, which keeps the insides soft while the tops become golden and crispy.

Yield: 12 biscuits

3 cups self-rising flour
1 teaspoon garlic powder
½ teaspoon onion powder
½ cup (1 stick, or 4 ounces) salted cold butter, cubed, plus 2 tablespoons salted butter, melted
2 cups shredded sharp cheddar cheese
1 cup whole buttermilk
1 teaspoon chopped fresh Italian parsley
¼ teaspoon garlic salt

Preheat the oven to 425°F. Butter the bottom and sides of a 10-inch cast-iron skillet.

In a medium-size mixing bowl, sift together the flour, garlic powder, and onion powder. Use a pastry blender or two forks to cut the cubed butter into the flour until it resembles cornmeal. Mix the cheddar cheese into the crumbs.

Make a well in the center and add the buttermilk. Mix the buttermilk into the dry ingredients gradually, using a fork. Mix until just fully moistened.

Use a 4-ounce ice-cream scoop to divide the dough, placing the biscuits side by side in the skillet.

Mix together the melted butter, parsley, and garlic salt. Lightly brush the tops of the biscuits, reserving some of the herbed butter for the tops at the end of baking.

Bake for 15 to 20 minutes, or until cooked through and golden. Broil at the end of baking to brown the tops further, if desired.

Brush with the reserved herbed butter and serve.

PULL-APART GARLIC PARMESAN-HERB KNOTS

This recipe is a spin-off of one of the most popular recipes on my website, my Garlic Parmesan Pull-Apart Bread. This variation is my go-to when I'm preparing a special meal for family and friends or entertaining guests. The buttery garlic coating is to die for, making it a stellar choice to serve with any meal.

Yield: 16 knots

16 frozen dinner yeast roll dough balls

½ cup (1 stick, 4 ounces) salted butter, melted

1 teaspoon dried parsley

2 garlic cloves, mashed and finely minced

3 tablespoons grated Parmesan cheese

1 teaspoon dried Italian seasoning or oregano

½ teaspoon garlic powder

½ teaspoon onion powder

Place the frozen dough rounds on waxed paper. Thaw on the counter for 20 to 30 minutes. The dough rounds should be thawed but still cold.

Butter a 9-inch springform pan. Set aside.

In a small bowl, mix together the melted butter, parsley, and garlic.

On a plate, sift together the Parmesan cheese, Italian seasoning, garlic powder, and onion powder.

On a nonstick surface, roll each of the dough rounds into a 6-inch rope. Tie into a knot, tucking the ends under.

Brush with garlic butter on all sides, then sprinkle with the seasoned Parmesan mixture. Reserve any unused garlic butter to brush on top at the end of baking.

Place side by side in the prepared pan. Repeat until all of the knots have been coated and placed in the pan.

Cover with plastic wrap and place in a draft-free area. Allow to rise until doubled, about 1½ to 2 hours.

Preheat the oven to 375°F. Remove the plastic wrap from the pan.

Bake for 22 to 25 minutes, or until golden. Brush the tops with the reserved garlic butter while warm.

Pull apart and enjoy.

SOUTHERN SKILLET CORN BREAD

If you'd like to start a spirited discussion in a room full of Southern cooks, ask whether corn bread should be sweet or savory. It never ceases to amaze me how strongly people disagree on this subject. Traditional corn bread usually begins with bacon drippings and is made using all cornmeal and tends to be savory in flavor. That said, there is no shortage of sweet or spicy versions and a plethora of other variations available. My rule of thumb is, if those eating the corn bread like the flavor, that ends the debate. This traditional skillet corn bread is savory in flavor and one you'll revisit time and time again.

Yield: 8 wedges corn bread

2 tablespoons bacon drippings
2 cups yellow self-rising cornmeal
1½ cups whole buttermilk
4 tablespoons salted butter, melted
1 large egg, beaten
Sweet cream butter, for serving

Preheat the oven to 425°F. Place the bacon drippings in an 8-inch cast-iron skillet and place the skillet into the oven while it preheats.

Whisk together the cornmeal, buttermilk, melted butter, and egg.

Swirl the bacon drippings around the skillet, coating the sides and bottom. Pour the corn bread batter into the hot skillet.

Bake for 20 to 25 minutes, or until golden.

Serve hot slathered with sweet cream butter.

JALAPEÑO PEPPER JACK CORN BREAD

This kicked-up corn bread is a feast for the senses and goes perfectly with a bowl of pinto beans, soup, or chili. The addition of cream-style corn tames the spice in the diced jalapeño and provides a balance in flavor that is undeniably satisfying.

Yield: 9 squares corn bread

2 cups yellow self-rising cornmeal

1 (15-ounce) can cream-style corn

½ cup (1 stick, 4 ounces) salted butter, melted

½ cup seeded and diced red bell pepper

1 small jalapeño pepper, seeded and diced

⅓ cup whole buttermilk

1 large egg, lightly beaten

1 teaspoon garlic salt

1 teaspoon onion powder

2 cups shredded pepper Jack cheese

Preheat the oven to 375°F. Spray a 9-inch square baking dish with cooking spray.

Whisk together the cornmeal, corn, melted butter, bell pepper, jalapeño pepper, buttermilk, egg, garlic salt, and onion powder until fully combined and moistened. Mix in the shredded pepper Jack cheese by hand.

Pour into the prepared baking dish. Bake for 30 to 35 minutes, or until golden and a toothpick inserted into the center shows moist crumbs.

Serve immediately.

NO-FAIL PIZZA DOUGH

Making homemade pizza dough isn't as difficult as you may think. Pizza dough also keeps well in the fridge; if you'd like to make it in advance, then pull it out for an interactive meal: Gather various toppings, set up a toppings bar, and let everyone get in on the pizza making fun. I recommend using bread flour for the crunch it gives to the crust, but if you prefer a chewier texture, substituting the same amount of all-purpose flour will work.

Yield: 2 (16-inch) pizza crusts

5 cups bread flour
2 (¼-ounce) envelopes rapid-rise dry yeast
1 tablespoon salt
1 tablespoon granulated sugar
2 cups warm water (110°–115°F), plus more if needed
3 tablespoons olive oil, divided

In the bowl of a stand mixer fitted with a dough hook, mix together the bread flour, yeast, salt, and sugar.

While the mixer is running, drizzle in the warm water mixed with 2 tablespoons of the olive oil. If needed, add additional warm water 1 tablespoon at a time until the dough is fully moistened. Knead until the dough comes together and pulls away from the sides of the bowl.

Turn out onto a nonstick surface and knead by hand 8 to 10 times, or until the dough is smooth and elastic.

Return the dough to the bowl and drizzle with the remaining tablespoon of olive oil. Turn to coat all sides. Cover and allow to rise for 1 hour, or until doubled.

Divide the dough in half to make two 16-inch pizzas. Top with your favorite pizza toppings and bake in a preheated 450°F oven for about 10 to 15 minutes, or until the crust is golden.

CLASSIC HUSHPUPPIES

In the South we love our fish fries. It would be remiss of a host or hostess to not include these bite-size nuggets of crispy fried corn bread to accompany the entrée. Serve these with a side of sweet cream butter and a drizzle of honey and they're nearly elevated to the status of a dessert.

Yield: About 25 hushpuppies

1 cup plain yellow cornmeal

1 cup all-purpose flour

⅓ cup granulated sugar

1 tablespoon baking powder

½ teaspoon baking soda

1½ teaspoons seafood seasoning, plus
      more for serving

1 teaspoon salt

1½ teaspoons granulated garlic

½ teaspoon onion powder

1 large egg, beaten

1 cup whole buttermilk

1 medium-size sweet onion, finely
      diced

Peanut oil, for frying

Butter and honey, for serving

Sift together the cornmeal, flour, sugar, baking powder, baking soda, seafood seasoning, salt, granulated garlic, and onion powder.

In a separate bowl whisk together the egg and buttermilk. Add the buttermilk mixture to the dry ingredients, and then stir in the onion. Mix until fully moistened. Allow the batter to rest on the counter while the oil heats.

In a large, deep pot, heat 4 inches of the oil to 350°F. Using a tablespoon or a 2-ounce ice-cream scoop to divide the batter, fry in batches, carefully dropping the batter into the hot oil. Cook for around 4 minutes, turning as needed for even browning. Transfer with a slotted spoon to paper towels to drain.

Season the hushpuppies lightly with additional seafood seasoning immediately after removing from the oil. Keep warm in a 250°F oven between batches, if desired.

Serve the hushpuppies warm as is or with a side of butter and a drizzle of honey.

SQUASH HUSHPUPPIES

This tasty variation on classic hushpuppies comes in handy in the summertime when yellow squash comes into season with a vengeance. You can serve these with any meal, but they go particularly well with a seafood dinner or a bowl of soup, or served with a spicy dip as an appetizer.

Yield: About 20 hushpuppies

2 cups (¼-inch-cubed) yellow squash

Peanut oil, for frying

1 cup self-rising yellow cornmeal

¼ cup all-purpose flour

1½ teaspoons seasoned salt, plus more for serving

1 teaspoon garlic powder

¼ teaspoon freshly ground black pepper

¼ teaspoon ground cumin

⅛ teaspoon cayenne pepper

1 cup whole buttermilk

1 large egg, beaten

½ cup finely chopped green onion

Steam the cubed squash for 6 to 8 minutes, or until fork-tender. Set aside to cool slightly.

In a large, deep pot, heat 4 inches of peanut oil to between 350° and 360°F. Line a baking sheet with paper towels. Set aside.

Sift together the cornmeal, flour, seasoned salt, garlic powder, black pepper, cumin, and cayenne.

In a separate bowl, whisk together the buttermilk and egg.

Add the squash and green onion to the wet ingredients. Add the wet ingredients to the sifted dry ingredients. Mix until fully moistened.

Using a 2-ounce ice-cream scoop or a tablespoon, carefully drop the batter into the oil. Fry for 3 to 4 minutes, until golden on both sides, turning as needed.

Use a slotted spoon to remove from the oil to the paper towel–lined baking sheet. Season lightly with additional seasoned salt.

Serve immediately.

Mouthwatering Side Dishes & Salads

The warm climate we enjoy in the South allows for longer garden growing seasons. In turn, Southerners will often happily make a meal out of vegetables alone. From roadside diners to white tablecloth-dining establishments, you'd be hard pressed to find a menu without a featured vegetable plate. It's not just a passing fad or the latest rage— it's a bona fide love affair that's here to stay.

Every generation of my family grew its own produce that was harvested at its peak and prepared to freeze or can for later use. It was a savvy way to feed and nourish a family well on a budget and enjoy fresh garden bounty year-round. Homegrown vegetables and legumes were celebrated. I have vivid memories during my childhood of at least one day of the week set aside for serving pinto beans and corn bread. On the side we might have had a simple salad consisting of cucumbers and tomatoes, or collard greens, hand-grated coleslaw made from home-grown cabbage, or sweet, freshly picked corn on the cob.

I continue to love the classic side dishes that I grew up eating. However, I also firmly believe there's always room for forward thinking and an opportunity to give some of these classics an updated twist.

BLT MACARONI SALAD

This fun take on pasta salad combines the flavors of a classic BLT with creamy macaroni salad. It's chock-full of crispy bacon, tomatoes, and crunchy green leaf lettuce, plus a tangy dressing. It's a fusion macaroni salad that takes BLTs to a whole new level.

Yield: 10 servings

1 (16-ounce) box elbow macaroni
1½ cups real mayonnaise, plus more if needed
¾ cup sour cream
3 tablespoons granulated sugar
2 tablespoons cider vinegar
1½ teaspoons celery salt
1½ teaspoons onion powder
1½ teaspoons garlic powder
½ teaspoon smoked paprika
¼ teaspoon dried dill
Freshly ground black pepper
5 green onions, thinly sliced, plus more for serving
4 Roma tomatoes, seeded and diced
2 cups loosely packed, thinly sliced green leaf lettuce
½ pound bacon, cooked and crumbled, plus more for serving

Cook the elbow macaroni in salted water per the package instructions until al dente. Drain well.

In a large mixing bowl, whisk together the mayonnaise, sour cream, sugar, vinegar, celery salt, onion powder, garlic powder, smoked paprika, dill, and pepper to taste.

Add the drained macaroni, green onions, and tomatoes. Mix until evenly distributed, then cover and chill.

Just before serving, add the lettuce and bacon. Mix well. Taste and adjust the creaminess of the dressing, adding more mayonnaise and adjusting the seasonings, if needed.

Garnish with additional bacon and green onion.

Store chilled.

SLOW-COOKED 3-BEAN COWBOY BEANS

Cowboy beans are a traditional Southwestern dish that pays homage to the type of food cowboys would have eaten on the trail. It's evolved into a beloved potluck classic and it seems everyone has his or her own little twist and flavor combinations. There's plenty of smoky bacon and ground beef, making it hearty and satisfying. After browning the ground beef on the stovetop, mix everything together and let the slow cooker do the rest.

Yield: 16 servings

½ pound bacon

1 medium-size sweet onion, diced

1 small red bell pepper, seeded and diced

1 small poblano pepper, seeded and diced

3 garlic cloves, minced

1 pound ground sirloin

1 teaspoon seasoned salt

½ teaspoon freshly ground black pepper

2 (16-ounce) cans pinto beans, drained and rinsed

1 (16-ounce) can light red kidney beans, drained and rinsed

1 (16-ounce) can black beans, drained and rinsed

1 cup honey barbecue sauce

⅓ cup packed light brown sugar

1 tablespoon barbecue seasoning

1 tablespoon dark chili powder

1 tablespoon spicy brown mustard

2 teaspoons ground cumin

Bacon crumbles, for serving (optional)

Spray the bottom and sides of an oval 6-quart slow cooker with cooking spray.

In a large skillet, cook the bacon. Transfer to paper towels to drain and reserve 4 tablespoons of the drippings in the skillet. Discard or freeze the rest of the drippings.

Sauté the onion, bell pepper, and poblano pepper in the bacon drippings over medium-high for 3 to 5 minutes, or until softened and beginning to brown. Add the garlic and cook for 1 minute.

Add the ground sirloin to the skillet. Sprinkle with the seasoned salt and black pepper. Cook for 10 minutes, or until no pink remains.

Drain any excess fat from the pan, then add all the remaining ingredients, except the optional bacon crumbles. Mix well.

Pour the bean mixture into the prepared slow cooker.

Cook on HIGH for 2 to 3 hours or on LOW for 4 to 5 hours.

Stir well before serving and sprinkle with additional bacon crumbles, if desired.

GREEN BEANS AND RED POTATOES WITH VIDALIA ONION AND BACON

Green beans and potatoes cooked together are a classic match and one that's complementary to most any meal. These fresh green beans are dressed up with smoky bacon and sweet Vidalia onion, making them company worthy but easy enough for any day of the week.

Yield: 8 servings

5 slices center-cut bacon

1 small Vidalia onion, diced

2 pounds whole green beans, ends removed

1½ cups low-sodium chicken stock

2 teaspoons garlic salt, divided

½ teaspoon freshly ground black pepper, divided

2 pounds small red potatoes, halved

2 tablespoons salted butter, cubed

In a large pot over medium-high heat, cook the bacon until crispy. Transfer with a slotted spoon to paper towels to drain and crumble. Reserve 4 tablespoons of the bacon drippings in the pot.

Add the onion to the drippings. Cook for 2 to 3 minutes, or until softened. Add the green beans, chicken stock, 1 teaspoon of the garlic salt, and ¼ teaspoon of the pepper. Stir well and cover. Lower the heat and simmer for 30 minutes.

After 30 minutes, sprinkle the green beans with ½ teaspoon of the garlic salt. Arrange the halved potatoes over the green beans.

Dot the potatoes with the butter and season with the remaining ¼ teaspoon of garlic salt and remaining ¼ teaspoon of pepper. Cover and simmer for an additional 30 minutes, or until the potatoes are fork-tender. Stir gently at the end of cooking to evenly distribute.

To serve, transfer to a serving dish and sprinkle with the crumbled bacon. Serve immediately.

GREEN CHILE SWEET CORN CASSEROLE

This comforting casserole is a cross between corn pudding and corn bread. The cream-style corn and cheddar cheese combine to give it a decadent creamy texture. The mild green chiles cut through the richness, making this dish suitable to be paired with most any entrée that you would regularly serve with corn or corn bread as the complementary side.

Yield: 10 servings

1 (15-ounce) can cream-style corn
1 (15-ounce) can corn, drained
1 (8-ounce) box yellow corn muffin mix
4 ounces diced green chiles
½ cup (1 stick, or 4 ounces) salted
    butter, melted
¼ cup milk
2 large eggs, beaten
2 teaspoons chopped chives
1 teaspoon garlic powder
2 cups shredded sharp cheddar
    cheese, divided

Preheat the oven to 350°F. Spray a 10-inch round, deep baking dish with cooking spray. Set aside.

In a medium-size mixing bowl, whisk together all the ingredients, except the cheddar cheese. Whisk until fully combined.

Use a large spoon or spatula to mix in 1 cup of the cheddar cheese.

Pour into the prepared baking dish and top with the remaining cup of cheddar cheese.

Bake, checking the center with a toothpick at 40 minutes and covering loosely with foil to prevent overbrowning if the center isn't cooked through. Bake for 10 to 20 more minutes, or until the center is set when gently shaken.

Let rest on the counter for 10 minutes before serving.

BROCCOLI CHEDDAR RICE CASSEROLE

This cheesy potluck favorite is comfort food at its best. Take it up a notch by adding chopped chicken and it becomes a one-dish meal that's budget friendly, too. When steaming the broccoli, make an effort to slightly undercook it. This helps ensure the florets will maintain their texture and not become too soft while baking with the remaining ingredients.

Yield: 10 servings

4 cups broccoli florets, steamed until crisp-tender
1 (3-ounce) package chicken-flavored rice, cooked
2 cups shredded sharp cheddar cheese, divided
1 (10¾-ounce) can cream of celery soup
1 (10¾-ounce) can cheddar cheese soup
⅓ cup real mayonnaise
6 tablespoons salted butter, melted, divided
1 large egg, beaten
1 small sweet onion, finely diced
1½ teaspoons garlic salt
½ teaspoon freshly ground black pepper
¼ teaspoon dry mustard
18 buttery round crackers, crushed

Preheat the oven to 350°F. Spray a 10 × 10-inch baking dish with cooking spray. Set aside.

In a medium-size mixing bowl, mix together the steamed broccoli florets, cooked chicken-flavored rice, 1½ cups of the cheddar cheese, celery soup, cheddar cheese soup, mayonnaise, 4 tablespoons of the melted butter, egg, onion, garlic salt, pepper, and mustard. Mix well.

Spread the broccoli mixture in the prepared baking dish and sprinkle the top with the remaining ½ cup of cheddar cheese.

Mix the remaining 2 tablespoons of melted butter with the cracker crumbs. Sprinkle over the cheese.

Bake for 35 to 40 minutes, or until golden and bubbly.

Serve immediately.

GOOEY 5-CHEESE MACARONI AND CHEESE

Endlessly versatile and universally loved, creamy macaroni and cheese can only be described one way. *Marvelous.* Perhaps when it comes to this recipe, no words are needed at all. Here I'm revealing my secret ingredient for making the creamiest, dreamiest macaroni and cheese sauce you've ever had the pleasure of experiencing. It's a gooey cheese-laden meal in itself and I declare that it deserves to be elevated to the status of its own food group. Amen.

Yield: 12 servings

2 cups elbow macaroni

½ cup (1 stick, or 4 ounces) salted
    butter, divided

⅓ cup all-purpose flour

1 teaspoon salt

½ teaspoon freshly ground black
    pepper

½ teaspoon Dijon mustard

Pinch of ground nutmeg

4 cups whole milk

3 ounces cream cheese, softened
    and cubed

2 cups shredded sharp white
    cheddar cheese

2 cups shredded medium yellow
    cheddar cheese

2 cups shredded mozzarella cheese

1 cup panko breadcrumbs

1 tablespoon grated Parmesan cheese

Preheat the oven to 350°F. Spray an 8 × 12-inch baking dish with cooking spray. Set aside.

Cook the elbow macaroni per the instructions on the package in salted water until al dente. Drain well.

Meanwhile, in a heavy-bottomed saucepan over medium-high heat, melt 6 tablespoons of the butter. Lower the heat to medium and add the flour. Stir until the flour is moistened and cook for 2 minutes, or until all of the flour lumps have dissolved.

Add the salt, pepper, mustard, and nutmeg. Mix well.

Increase the heat to high and begin to whisk in the milk. Whisk constantly until all of the roux has been incorporated and the milk begins to boil. Immediately lower the heat and allow the sauce to bubble gently for 5 minutes, stirring occasionally to prevent sticking.

Add the cream cheese. Whisk gently until the cream cheese has completely melted and the sauce is smooth. Turn off the heat.

In a bowl, mix together the cheddar cheeses and mozzarella cheese. Add half of the mixed cheeses to the cream cheese mixture. Stir until the added cheeses have melted.

Add the cooked macaroni to the cheese sauce, mixing until evenly coated. Pour half of the macaroni mixture into the prepared baking dish.

Sprinkle half of the remaining mixed cheeses over the first layer of macaroni. Pour the rest of the macaroni evenly on top. Sprinkle with the remaining mixed cheeses.

Melt the remaining 2 tablespoons of butter in a microwave-safe bowl. Toss with the breadcrumbs and Parmesan cheese. Sprinkle on top of the casserole.

Place in the oven and bake for 30 to 35 minutes, or until golden and bubbly around the edges. Let rest for 10 minutes on the counter before serving.

CREAMY GRUYÈRE PARMESAN GRITS

Grits are to Southerners what polenta is to Italians. While both Southern grits and polenta are made from stone-ground corn, the difference lies in the type of corn being used. Southern grits are ground from hominy. Hominy is the result of dried corn kernels that have been soaked in lye or lime and rinsed to remove the hull. When hominy is ground, the removal of the hull lends a finer texture. Polenta is ground from whole corn kernels, making it coarser, and it tends to be yellow in color. Southern grits can be white or yellow and at times boast other color variations.

For this recipe, I chose to use quick-cooking grits due to the ease of preparation and shorter cooking time. If time allows, stone-ground or coarsely ground grits are the proverbial gold standard but take much longer to cook. These creamy grits are slightly nutty in flavor with the addition of the Gruyère, and the Parmesan cheese gives them a salty bite. The savory flavor makes them go particularly well with braised short ribs, shrimp, ham, or beef stew.

Yield: 12 servings

3 cups low-sodium chicken stock, plus more as needed, to thin

3 cups whole milk

4 tablespoons salted butter

2 teaspoons garlic salt

2 cups quick-cooking grits

¼ cup grated Parmesan cheese

3 ounces cream cheese, softened

1 cup shredded Gruyère cheese

In a heavy-bottomed saucepan, bring the chicken stock, milk, butter, and garlic salt to a boil.

Whisking constantly, slowly add the grits. Adjust the temperature to low, cover, and simmer, stirring periodically to prevent sticking and adding additional chicken stock as needed to thin, for 20 to 25 minutes, or until all the liquid has been absorbed and the grits have softened.

At the end of cooking, add the Parmesan cheese and cream cheese. Stir until the cream cheese has completely melted.

Remove from the heat and mix in the Gruyère cheese by hand.

Serve immediately.

SLOW-COOKED CHEESY SCALLOPED POTATOES

Everyone loves potatoes. These scalloped potatoes are dreamy and made conveniently in a slow cooker. They're just what you need when the oven is tied up with other dishes or during warm summer months when turning the oven on isn't very appealing. You can serve these scalloped potatoes straight from the slow cooker or remove to a pretty platter instead. It doesn't matter how you choose to serve them; they're delightful to the very last spoonful.

Yield: 10 servings

1½ cups low-sodium chicken broth

1 (10¾-ounce) can cream of potato soup

4 ounces chive and onion cream cheese, softened

3 tablespoons grated Parmesan cheese

4 tablespoons salted butter, melted

1 teaspoon garlic powder

1 teaspoon salt

½ teaspoon freshly ground black pepper

¼ teaspoon dry mustard

3 pounds Yukon gold potatoes, sliced ¼ inch thick

1 small sweet onion, finely diced

3 cups shredded sharp white cheddar cheese

1 tablespoon chopped chives or green onion

2 slices bacon, cooked and crumbled

Liberally spray the bottom and sides of an oval 6-quart slow cooker with cooking spray.

Pour the chicken stock, potato soup, cream cheese, Parmesan cheese, melted butter, garlic powder, salt, pepper, and mustard into a stand blender. Blend until the sauce is fully combined and smooth.

Begin by layering one-third of the sliced potatoes on the bottom of the slow cooker. Sprinkle with one-third of the diced onion. Drizzle with one-third of the sauce and sprinkle with one-third of the cheddar cheese (see Cook's Note). Repeat the layers, ending with the cheese.

Cover the opening of the slow cooker with doubled paper towels, then place the lid firmly on top.

Cook on the HIGH setting for 3 to 4 hours, or on LOW for 6 to 7 hours. Test the potatoes with a fork for tenderness. When done, remove the crock from the slow cooker, sprinkle with chopped chives and crumbled bacon and allow to rest uncovered for 10 minutes before serving.

COOK'S NOTE:
Eight ounces cubed ham may be added to the layers, one-third at a time, after adding the onion layer, if desired.

OVEN-ROASTED GARLIC AND HERB CORN ON THE COB

Sweet corn on the cob needs little help to make it taste delicious; it was designed to grow that way all on its own. Design and a little help from above, of course. On special occasions, this oven-roasted corn is a fabulous way to make grown-up seasoned corn for a crowd with very little effort. It's side-dish perfection when corn is in season and ideal for a backyard barbecue.

Yield: 8 servings

6 tablespoons salted butter, at room temperature
1 tablespoon chopped fresh Italian parsley
1 teaspoon garlic salt
¼ teaspoon onion powder
¼ teaspoon freshly ground black pepper
8 corn on the cob, husks and silk removed

Preheat the oven to 425°F. Line a 10 × 15-inch jelly-roll pan or rimmed baking pan with heavy-duty aluminum foil. Coat liberally with cooking spray.

Mix together the butter, parsley, garlic salt, onion powder, and pepper.

Slather the corn on all sides with half of the seasoned butter. Lay side by side on the prepared baking sheet. Cover loosely with foil.

Bake, turning occasionally, for 25 minutes, or until tender.

Change the oven setting to BROIL. Broil, uncovered, for 3 to 5 minutes, to char slightly.

Brush with the remaining seasoned butter and serve.

BROWNED BUTTER LIMA BEANS AND HAM

Lima beans and butter beans are considered both a side dish and an entrée in the South. They often start with bacon drippings, but I wanted to shake things up a little and use browned butter instead. The browned butter adds a nuttiness to the overall flavor, making this simple dish *simply delicious*.

Yield: 10 servings

½ cup (1 stick, or 4 ounces) salted butter

1 (32-ounce) package frozen baby lima beans

1 (14-ounce) can low-sodium chicken stock

½ pound smoked ham, cubed

1½ teaspoons garlic salt

½ teaspoon freshly ground black pepper

In a medium-size heavy bottomed saucepan, melt the butter. Cook on medium heat for 5 to 7 minutes, or until the milk solids have turned a caramel color and the butter has browned.

Add the frozen lima beans, chicken stock, ham, garlic salt, and pepper to the browned butter. Stir well and bring to a boil, then lower the heat to medium and simmer, partially covered with an offset lid, for 20 minutes, or until the beans are tender.

Let rest, uncovered, for 5 to 10 minutes, then serve.

HOMESTYLE POTATO SALAD

This homestyle potato salad, which boasts a tangy and slightly sweet homemade dressing, is filled with sweet pickle cubes, chopped boiled eggs, and buttery Yukon gold potatoes. It's delightful served warm in the cool weather months or chilled for a backyard family picnic. It's a sure-fire crowd-pleaser any time of year.

Yield: 10 servings

3 pounds Yukon gold potatoes, cut into 1-inch cubes
1¼ cups real mayonnaise
¼ cup sour cream
3 tablespoons granulated sugar
1 tablespoon spicy brown mustard
1 teaspoon yellow mustard
1 teaspoon salt
1 teaspoon onion powder
1 teaspoon cider vinegar
1 teaspoon chopped fresh dill
½ teaspoon freshly ground black pepper
½ teaspoon celery seeds
4 large hard-boiled eggs
5 green onions, thinly sliced, divided

Cook the cubed potatoes in salted water for 10 to 12 minutes, or until fork-tender. Drain well and let cool slightly.

In a large mixing bowl, whisk together the mayonnaise, sour cream, sugar, brown mustard, yellow mustard, salt, onion powder, vinegar, dill, pepper, and celery seeds until fully combined.

Peel and chop three of the hard-boiled eggs for the salad, slicing and reserving the remaining whole egg for garnish.

Gently toss the potatoes with the dressing, chopped hard-boiled eggs, and green onions, reserving 2 tablespoons of green onion for garnish.

Serve warm or chilled. If chilling, leave uncovered until completely cool (see Cook's Note), then stir and cover.

Transfer to a serving dish and garnish with the reserved hard-boiled egg slices and green onions just before serving.

COOK'S NOTE:
If you cover this salad before it has cooled, condensation may form on the lid and drip onto the potato salad, potentially causing the dressing to break down and become watery. I recommend that you let the salad cool completely, and then cover tightly for storage.

SOUR CREAM CUCUMBER AND ONION SALAD

This easy summer salad is dressed with a slightly sweet sour cream dressing. It can be prepared in a jiffy but must be chilled thoroughly before serving to allow the flavors to fully combine.

Yield: 6 servings

8 ounces sour cream

2 tablespoons cider vinegar

2 tablespoons granulated sugar or other sweetener of choice

1 teaspoon chopped fresh dill

1 teaspoon garlic salt

½ teaspoon onion powder

¼ teaspoon freshly ground black pepper

⅛ teaspoon celery seeds

1 English cucumber, thinly sliced

1 small sweet onion, thinly sliced

In a medium-size mixing bowl, whisk together the sour cream, vinegar, sugar, dill, garlic salt, onion powder, pepper, and celery seeds.

Add the cucumber and onion slices to the dressing. Stir gently to combine.

Cover and chill for at least 4 hours.

DILL DEVILED EGGS

It wouldn't be a family or holiday gathering without a platter of deviled eggs on the table. This easy recipe is how my Mom taught me to make deviled eggs and it is the one I return to over and over again. It boasts a slightly sweet filling to balance the sharp tang of the fresh dill.

When it comes to deviled eggs, the variations and filling options are infinite. Some filling choices may even seem controversial to deviled egg purists. That said, it doesn't matter how you fill them; they all begin the same way: Simmer the eggs in lightly salted water for 10 minutes, remove from the heat and let cool slightly so they're easier to handle, and then get crackin'.

Yield: 12 deviled eggs

8 large eggs
3 heaping tablespoons real
    mayonnaise
2 tablespoons sweet pickle relish
2 teaspoons spicy brown or yellow
    mustard
1 teaspoon chopped fresh dill, plus
    more for garnish
1 teaspoon granulated sugar
½ teaspoon salt
¼ teaspoon black pepper
Smoked paprika, for garnish

Place the eggs in a single layer in a deep pot. Cover with water, allowing at least 1 inch coverage above the eggs. Bring the eggs to a rolling boil. Turn off the heat and cover. Allow to sit on the burner for 10 to 12 minutes.

Drain the hot water and cover the eggs with cold water. Peel the eggs, and slice in half. Transfer all the yolks to a mixing bowl.

To make the filling, use a fork to finely mash together the egg yolks and the cooked whites of two of the eggs (four egg white halves). Add the mayonnaise, pickle relish, mustard, dill, sugar, salt, and pepper. Mix until fully combined. Taste and adjust the salt, if needed.

Divide the egg filling equally among the remaining egg halves. Sprinkle the tops with smoked paprika and garnish with a sprig of dill.

Chill thoroughly.

LAYERED CORN BREAD SALAD

This five-star salad makes an exquisite edible centerpiece. Layers of crumbled corn bread, crispy bacon, pinto beans, corn, bell peppers, cherry tomatoes, green onion, and cheddar cheese are drizzled with a creamy ranch dressing. It not only packs loads of flavor but has the "wow" factor, too. It's perfect for summer entertaining or you can serve it with tortilla chips as a dip. Either way, it's sure to be a hit at your next fiesta or tailgating party.

Yield: 12 servings

1 recipe Southern Skillet Corn Bread (page 86)

1 recipe Homemade Buttermilk Ranch Dressing (page 122)

8 ounces sharp cheddar cheese, shredded

1 red bell pepper, seeded and diced

1 green bell pepper, seeded and diced

1 pound bacon, cooked and crumbled

1 (15-ounce) can pinto beans, drained and rinsed

10 green onions, thinly sliced

1 pint cherry tomatoes, halved

1 (15-ounce) can corn with peppers, drained

One day in advance, bake the corn bread, let cool, and crumble roughly. Prepare the dressing and chill thoroughly.

Divide the corn bread and cheddar cheese into thirds. Divide the remaining ingredients in half, setting aside 2 tablespoons of green onions for garnish.

To assemble, in a trifle bowl or other large, clear glass bowl, layer one-third of the corn bread, one-third of the cheddar cheese, and half of the red bell pepper, green bell pepper, crumbled bacon, pinto beans, green onions, cherry tomatoes, and corn, in that order. Drizzle with half of the ranch dressing.

Repeat: one-third of the corn bread, one-third of the cheddar cheese, and the remaining half of the red bell pepper, green bell pepper, bacon, pinto beans, green onions, and corn, ending with the dressing. Garnish with the remaining cheddar cheese, corn bread crumbles, green onions, and cherry tomatoes.

Cover with plastic wrap and chill overnight.

HOMEMADE BUTTERMILK RANCH DRESSING

Naturally, we all reach for prepared bottled salad dressings when we're in a time crunch. When time isn't an issue, I much prefer making my own dressings and dips from scratch. This flavorful homemade ranch dressing can be turned into a dip just by adding a little more mayonnaise, making it a versatile choice, too. Be certain to prepare this dressing in advance to give the flavors time to combine and mellow.

Yield: 2 cups dressing

1½ cups whole buttermilk
⅔ cup real mayonnaise
1 tablespoon fresh chopped chives
1 teaspoon garlic salt
1 teaspoon garlic powder
1 teaspoon onion powder
1 teaspoon lemon pepper
½ teaspoon freshly ground black
    pepper
½ teaspoon granulated sugar
¼ teaspoon dried dill

Whisk together all the ingredients and pour into a mason jar. Seal tightly and chill thoroughly. Shake well prior to serving.

This dressing may be made up to 1 week in advance.

Store chilled.

CREAMY COLESLAW

Coleslaw is a vegetable salad commonly served alongside hot dogs or fried chicken, piled high on top of pulled pork barbecue sandwiches, or served with a bowl of pinto beans and corn bread. The name is derived from the Dutch word *koolsla*, which simply means "cabbage salad."

Americans have been eating coleslaw since the 1700s and by my family for as long as I can remember. For the best results, use the freshest ingredients and chill thoroughly to allow the flavors of the dressing and vegetables to marry before serving.

Yield: 12 servings

4 tablespoons salted butter
½ cup white distilled vinegar
1½ tablespoons all-purpose flour
1 tablespoon freshly squeezed lemon
    juice
1 teaspoon onion powder
½ teaspoon celery salt
½ teaspoon freshly ground white
    pepper
1 large egg yolk, beaten
1 cup granulated sugar
2 (16-ounce) bags tricolor deli-style
    coleslaw mix
4 green onions, chopped

Melt the butter over medium heat in a heavy-bottomed saucepan. Whisk in the vinegar. Whisk in the flour, lemon juice, onion powder, celery salt, and white pepper. Continue to whisk until the ingredients are fully incorporated.

In a small bowl, temper the egg yolk by adding 2 tablespoons of the warm vinegar liquid. While whisking, slowly drizzle the egg yolk mixture into the hot vinegar mixture to cook. Cook on low heat for 1 to 2 minutes.

Remove from the heat and beat in the sugar. Beat for 2 minutes, or until the dressing has thickened and is light yellow in color. Let cool.

In a large mixing bowl, toss the coleslaw mix, green onions, and the cooled dressing. Chill for at least 4 hours before serving

STRAWBERRY SALAD WITH BACON, BLUE CHEESE, AND CANDIED PECANS

This crisp fresh salad is a magnificent choice to serve as a light lunch or dinner. It can also be served as an impressive dinner entrée salad topped with grilled chicken, steak, or shrimp. Drizzle with the homemade sweet and tangy poppy seed vinaigrette to create a winning combination that works every single time.

Yield: 6 servings

Candied Pecans:
3 tablespoons salted butter
⅓ cup packed light brown sugar
1 tablespoon light corn syrup
¼ teaspoon salt
1 cup pecan halves

Salad:
10 ounces spring mix baby greens
1 quart fresh strawberries, hulled and halved
½ pound bacon, cooked and crumbled
2 ounces crumbled blue cheese
Poppy Seed Vinaigrette (recipe follows)

To make the candied pecans: In a nonstick skillet over medium-high heat, melt the butter. Add the brown sugar, corn syrup, and salt.

Bring to a simmer and cook, stirring constantly, for 2 minutes. Lower the heat to medium. Add the pecan halves and cook for 1 additional minute, or until all the pecans are evenly coated.

Remove from the heat and spread on parchment paper to cool, then break apart.

To make the salad: Layer the greens, strawberry halves, bacon crumbles, blue cheese, and candied pecans in a large salad bowl. Chill.

Serve drizzled with the Poppy Seed Vinaigrette.

POPPY SEED VINAIGRETTE

Yield: 1½ cups vinaigrette

⅓ cup cider vinegar
½ cup granulated sugar
1 finely minced shallot, or ¼ cup red onion
1½ teaspoons dry mustard
1½ teaspoons coarse sea salt
1½ teaspoons poppy seeds
1 cup canola oil

Combine the vinegar, sugar, shallot, mustard, and salt in a blender. Purée for 20 to 30 seconds, or until the mixture is smooth.

Remove the lid, reduce the speed of the blender, and add the poppy seeds. Slowly drizzle in the oil. Continue to blend until the dressing emulsifies and thickens.

Chill until serving.

CUCUMBER TOMATO SALAD WITH AVOCADO, CHICKPEAS, AND WHITE BALSAMIC VINAIGRETTE

This easy Mediterranean-inspired salad deviates a bit from the beaten path with the addition of diced avocado. It's a splendid addition, if I say so myself. It's the kind of salad that's a welcome alternative from the norm served at any picnic or cookout. It could also be served as a light lunch or dinner on a sultry Southern evening.

Yield: 6 servings

1 English cucumber, cubed

1 pint cherry tomatoes, halved

1 small red onion, thinly sliced

1 (14-ounce) can chickpeas, drained and rinsed

4 ounces feta cheese, crumbled

2 small avocados, peeled, pitted, and cubed

2 tablespoons chopped fresh Italian parsley

Place the cucumber, cherry tomatoes, red onion, and chickpeas in a mixing bowl. Toss with the White Balsamic Vinaigrette (recipe follows). Cover tightly and refrigerate for at least 2 hours.

Just before serving, toss the feta cheese, avocados, and parsley with the marinated vegetables. Taste and adjust the seasonings, if needed.

Serve immediately.

WHITE BALSAMIC VINAIGRETTE

⅓ cup olive oil

¼ cup white balsamic vinegar

2 tablespoons freshly squeezed lemon juice

2 tablespoons granulated sugar

1 teaspoon dried Italian seasoning

1 teaspoon salt

1 teaspoon garlic powder

½ teaspoon freshly ground black pepper

¼ teaspoon red pepper flakes

Whisk together the ingredients for the vinaigrette.

The Main Attraction

While I was growing up, my parents' lives and work were centered on church. Due to this I attended many potluck get-togethers and meals. I grew to love those types of events dearly. Potlucks, by their very nature, encourage a sense of community as friends and neighbors bring their very best dishes to share with one another. Long tables draped with white tablecloths were filled with a variety of mouthwatering main-dish casseroles, steaming side dishes, fresh homemade breads, and slow cooker delights. The choices were mind-boggling. Then there was the incredible desserts table, bursting with an astounding assortment of drool-worthy treats. Both the aroma and anticipation of the meal made it difficult to concentrate on anything else. The community always rallied for one of those events where they could experience lively chatter, laughter, and friendly conversation all served around a community table with a heaping helping of hospitality.

The dishes that are typically served at potluck and covered-dish meals are initially perfected in everyday family meals at home. While I love fine dining, there's nothing quite like a homemade meal with that special ingredient that money can't buy. Whether a first-time cook or a seasoned hostess, we all need a little inspiration from time to time. Turn the main dish into the main attraction and you'll only have to ring the dinner bell once.

CAST-IRON BUTTERMILK FRIED CHICKEN

While I'm not always crazy about the stereotypes that are often associated with food in the South, we do know a thing or two about how to make the world's greatest fried chicken. All Southern cooks have their own special technique often passed to them by family cooks who've been frying chicken for decades.

When I'm asked the ultimate "secret" to Southern fried chicken, I'm not certain there is a definitive answer. Just like bread making, perfecting the art of frying chicken takes practice. I was taught to begin the process of preparing the chicken the night before and placing the chicken pieces in a buttermilk brine. That would be whole buttermilk, mind you: the kind that contains *all* of the butter fat. The dredging station is the next step, making sure you thoughtfully add appropriate amounts of seasoning to each and every layer. More specifically you must season the chicken pieces, the flour, *and* the egg wash.

That said, there is something magical about shallow-frying chicken in cast iron. This was standard practice in my family and how both of my grandmothers made fried chicken and it's still the best. The cast-iron skillet keeps the oil at a constant temperature, which gives the chicken a supercrispy coating and nongreasy texture.

There are a few things to keep in mind: You should never crowd the chicken pieces in the skillet. If you do, the pieces won't cook evenly and will stick together. It's also helpful to have nearby a baking pan fitted with an oven-safe rack, to keep cooked pieces warm between batches. In addition, there will always be variables: You should consider the size of the chicken pieces, increasing the cooking time for larger pieces when needed and likewise decreasing the cooking time for smaller pieces.

Here's to the chicken-frying aficionado in us all.

Yield: 8 servings

1 chicken, cut into 8 pieces
3 cups whole buttermilk, divided
3 cups all-purpose flour
Seasoned salt
Freshly ground black pepper
1 teaspoon onion powder
1 teaspoon garlic powder
2 large eggs, beaten
1 teaspoon hot sauce
Peanut oil, for frying

To marinate: Rinse and pat dry the chicken pieces. Arrange in a single layer in a 9 × 13-inch baking dish and cover with 2 cups of the buttermilk. Cover with plastic wrap and refrigerate overnight, turning once.

To bread the chicken: On a plate or platter, mix together the flour, 2 teaspoons of seasoned salt, 1 teaspoon of pepper, and the onion powder and garlic powder.

In a wide, shallow bowl or dish, whisk the eggs with the remaining cup of buttermilk and the hot sauce.

Remove the chicken from the buttermilk marinade, shaking off any excess (discard the marinade). Season each chicken piece lightly with seasoned salt and pepper.

Dip each chicken piece into the seasoned flour, then into the egg wash, and back into the seasoned flour, then place on a waxed paper–lined baking sheet. Refrigerate for 30 minutes to 1 hour.

To fry the chicken: Preheat the oven to 225°F. Fit a baking rack into a jelly-roll pan or large, rimmed baking pan. Set aside.

Fill a 12-inch cast-iron skillet one-third full with peanut oil. Heat between 350° and 360°F. Maintain the oil temperature around 325°F while frying, but begin each batch at between 350° and 360°F.

Place a few pieces of chicken at a time into the hot oil, being careful not to overcrowd the skillet. The pieces should not touch. Start skin side down.

Cook, covered, for about 5 minutes. Uncover and continue to cook for 5 minutes.

Turn the chicken pieces and cook covered, for 5 minutes, then uncover and cook for an additional 5 to 10 minutes, or until the chicken has cooked through. Repeat this process, frying until the juices run clear. During the last 3 minutes, gently turn the pieces to crisp each side, if needed. Adjust the frying time, depending on the size of the chicken pieces.

To keep warm between batches, fit a rimmed baking pan with an oven-safe rack. Place the fried chicken pieces on the rack and into a 225°F oven to keep warm between batches.

Continue until all the chicken is fried.

Let rest on the counter for 10 minutes before serving.

COOK'S NOTE:
If the chicken is becoming golden brown and the juices are still pink, the chicken may be finished in a preheated 325°F oven. Bake for 10 to 15 minutes depending on the size of the pieces. Large breast pieces may take longer; and smaller pieces, less time. Adjust the time accordingly.

CHICKEN 'N' DUMPLINS

Down-home chicken 'n' dumplins can really hit the spot on a cool rainy day. This version comes together quickly, making it an option even on busy weekdays. The trick to keeping the dumplins tender is to keep the lid firmly in place while they're cooking. In around 30 minutes, this luscious comfort food classic is ready to eat . . . with a nap sure to follow.

Yield: 8 servings

3 cups roughly chopped cooked chicken

3 (14-ounce) cans low-sodium chicken stock

1 (10¾-ounce) can cream of celery soup

2 teaspoons poultry seasoning (see Cook's Note)

1 teaspoon salt

½ teaspoon freshly ground black pepper

½ teaspoon dried tarragon

½ teaspoon onion powder

¼ teaspoon garlic powder

¼ cup all-purpose flour

4 tablespoons salted butter, at room temperature

Dumplins:

½ cup salted (1 stick, or 4 ounces) cold butter, cubed

3 cups self-rising flour

1 cup whole buttermilk

Place the chicken, chicken stock, celery soup, poultry seasoning, salt, pepper, tarragon, onion powder, and garlic powder in a large pot over high heat and bring to a boil.

In a small bowl, mix together the flour and butter to form a paste. Whisk into the pot to thicken the broth.

To make the dumplins: Cut the butter into the flour, using a pastry blender or food processor, until the mixture resembles cornmeal. Using a fork, mix the buttermilk into the flour until it forms soft dough.

Using a 2-ounce ice-cream scoop or tablespoon, drop the dough into the boiling broth. Immediately lower the heat to a simmer and cover tightly. Allow to simmer for 25 minutes without lifting the lid.

Uncover and gently stir. Let rest, uncovered, for at least 5 minutes, to allow the broth to thicken.

COOK'S NOTE:

In place of poultry seasoning, you may use ½ teaspoon each of ground sage, ground marjoram, ground thyme, and ground rosemary.

CHICKEN AND BISCUIT COBBLER

This savory cobbler is tried-and-true comfort food. The rich homemade filling is prepared on the stovetop, then crowned with homemade garlic and cheddar–filled drop biscuits. Like any other cobbler, this savory version is baked until bubbly and then it's ready to serve. Move over centerpiece—this savory cobbler deserves to be the main attraction.

Yield: 6 servings

Filling:

4 tablespoons salted butter

1 medium-size sweet onion, diced

1 cup diced carrot

1 celery rib, diced

Seasoned salt

Freshly ground black pepper

2 garlic cloves, minced

⅓ cup all-purpose flour

3 cups low-sodium chicken stock

⅔ cup heavy cream

2 teaspoons poultry seasoning (see Cook's Note)

1 teaspoon dried tarragon

1 teaspoon lemon pepper

3 cups roughly chopped cooked chicken

½ cup frozen petite peas

Biscuits:

3 cups self-rising flour

1 tablespoon fresh chives

1 teaspoon garlic powder

1 cup shredded sharp cheddar cheese

2 cups heavy cream

Preheat the oven to 350°F. Spray a 9 × 13-inch baking dish with cooking spray. Set aside.

To make the filling: In a large skillet over low heat, heat the butter and add the onion, carrot, and celery. Season lightly with seasoned salt and pepper. Cook until the vegetables are softened and beginning to brown, about 8 minutes. Add the garlic and continue to cook for 1 minute, or until fragrant.

Sprinkle the flour over the cooked vegetables. Stir until all of the flour has absorbed the butter.

Whisk in the chicken stock and bring to a boil. Lower the heat and simmer for 3 minutes, or until thickened. Once thickened, add the cream, 2 teaspoons of seasoned salt, and the poultry seasoning, tarragon, lemon pepper, chicken, and peas. Stir until heated through, then remove from the heat. Adjust the pepper to taste. Pour into the prepared baking dish.

To make the biscuits: In a medium-size mixing bowl, sift together the flour, chives, and garlic powder. Add the cheddar cheese, mixing until evenly distributed. Make a well in the center and add the cream. Mix with a fork until the flour is fully moistened.

Use a 4-ounce ice-cream scoop to divide into 12 biscuits. Arrange on top of the filling.

Bake for 35 to 40 minutes, or until the filling is bubbly and the biscuits are cooked through and golden. Serve immediately.

COOK'S NOTE:
In place of poultry seasoning, you may use ½ teaspoon each of ground sage, ground marjoram, ground thyme, and ground rosemary.

ONE-POT SPANISH CHICKEN AND CHORIZO RICE

This amazing one-pot Spanish-inspired meal is as delicious as the colors are vibrant. It's a feast for the eyes and the senses. It involves several simple steps but is well worth the effort. The chicken pieces are rubbed with fragrant seasonings and then browned in the drippings from the chorizo sausage and simmered with onion, bell peppers, and rice until tender. It's a family-style meal that's company worthy.

Yield: 6 servings

Olive oil
2 teaspoons ground cumin
2 teaspoons paprika
1 teaspoon dried Italian seasoning
6 (6-ounce) bone-in chicken thighs
8 ounces ground chorizo sausage, casings removed
1 medium-size onion, diced
1 small green bell pepper, seeded and diced
1 small red bell pepper, seeded and diced
Seasoned salt
Freshly ground black pepper
3 garlic cloves, minced
1 (10-ounce) package saffron rice
3 cups low-sodium chicken stock
1 (14-ounce) can fire-roasted tomatoes
1 bay leaf
½ cup pimiento-stuffed green olives
2 tablespoons chopped fresh cilantro

Mix 2 tablespoons of olive oil with the cumin, paprika, and Italian seasoning. Rub over the chicken thighs and place in a resealable plastic bag. Chill for at least 2 hours or overnight.

When ready to cook, in a large skillet, cook the ground sausage in a couple drizzles of olive oil until no pink remains. Use a slotted spoon to remove from the pan.

Brown the chicken in the chorizo drippings for 2 minutes on each side. Remove from the pan.

Add the onion and bell peppers to the pan. Season lightly with seasoned salt and black pepper. Cook for 3 to 5 minutes, or until softened and beginning to brown. Add the garlic and cook for 1 minute longer, or until fragrant.

Add the rice, chicken stock, fire-roasted tomatoes, bay leaf, 1½ teaspoons of seasoned salt, and ¼ teaspoon of black pepper to the pan. Mix in the cooked chorizo. Stir well. Nestle the chicken pieces on top and cover tightly.

Simmer for 30 to 35 minutes, or until the rice is tender and the chicken has cooked through. Remove from the heat and let rest covered for 10 minutes.

To serve, remove the bay leaf and garnish with the green olives and cilantro.

SLOPPY JOES

Homestyle sloppy joes are incredibly versatile and are a great way to clean out your vegetable drawer. You can transform them easily by adding a few drops of hot sauce to give them a kick, or give them a South of the Border twist by adding taco seasoning and salsa. Sloppy joes are one of those tummy-filling meals that keeps your family happy and your budget on track.

Yield: 8 servings

1 medium-size sweet onion, diced

1 small green bell pepper, seeded and diced

1 small red bell pepper, seeded and diced

2 garlic cloves, minced

2 pounds lean ground beef or chicken

1 (15-ounce) can tomato sauce

1 cup ketchup

3 to 4 tablespoons light brown sugar

2 tablespoons Worcestershire sauce

1½ teaspoons seasoned salt

½ teaspoon freshly ground black pepper

½ teaspoon smoked paprika

½ teaspoon dry mustard

½ teaspoon dried oregano

8 kaiser rolls

Cheddar, American, or your favorite cheese, for topping (optional)

In a large skillet, heat a couple of drizzles of olive oil. Cook the onion and bell peppers for 3 to 5 minutes, or until softened and beginning to brown. Add the garlic. Cook for 1 minute, or until fragrant.

Add the ground meat to the pan. Cook until no pink remains. Drain any excess fat from the pan.

Add the tomato sauce, ketchup, brown sugar, Worcestershire sauce, seasoned salt, black pepper, smoked paprika, mustard, and oregano to the skillet. Mix well.

Simmer, uncovered, for 20 minutes, or until the sauce has reduced slightly and intensified in flavor. Taste and adjust the salt and pepper to your taste.

Serve on warm kaiser rolls topped with cheese, if desired.

FIESTA TACO CASSEROLE

Taco casserole is a hearty and filling crowd favorite. This version is filled with lean ground beef, seasoned tomatoes, kidney beans, and Colby-Jack cheese, making it perfect for a weekday meal or a casual game day soiree. Top this colorful casserole with your favorite taco toppings and it becomes a fiesta in a bowl.

Yield: 8 servings

1 medium-size onion, diced

1 small poblano pepper, seeded and diced

1 small red bell pepper, seeded and diced

3 garlic cloves, minced

Salt and freshly ground black pepper

2 pounds lean ground beef

1 (15-ounce) can chili-seasoned tomatoes

1 (15-ounce) can light red kidney beans, drained and rinsed

1 (10¾-ounce) can fiesta nacho cheese soup

1 (1.25-ounce) package taco seasoning

1 tablespoon dark chili powder

½ teaspoon Mexican oregano

2 cups shredded Colby-Jack cheese, divided

4 cups crushed nacho-flavored tortilla chips, divided

Sour cream, sliced green onions, and cherry tomatoes, for garnish

Preheat the oven to 350°F. Spray a 7 × 11-inch baking dish with cooking spray. Set aside.

In a large skillet, heat a couple of drizzles of olive oil. Cook the onion, poblano pepper, and bell pepper until softened and beginning to brown, 3 to 5 minutes. Add the garlic and cook for 1 minute, or until fragrant. Season with salt and black pepper to taste.

Add the ground beef to the skillet. Cook over medium-high heat for around 8 minutes, or until no pink remains. Drain any excess fat from the pan.

Add the chili-seasoned tomatoes, kidney beans, nacho cheese soup, taco seasoning, chili powder, and oregano to the skillet. Stir until the ingredients are evenly distributed and the soup has melted. Remove from the heat.

Pour half of the mixture into the prepared baking dish. Sprinkle with half of the Colby-Jack cheese and crushed tortilla chips. Cover the chips with the remaining filling, then the remaining cheese, ending with the remaining tortilla chips.

Bake for 30 minutes. Serve immediately, garnished with sour cream, green onions, and cherry tomatoes.

SLOW COOKER BRAISED POT ROAST WITH BROWN GRAVY AND VEGETABLES

There's nothing better than coming home from a long day to have dinner ready and waiting for you. In particular, when the house is filled with the comforting aroma of tender pot roast and vegetables. It makes you glad to be home. The beef is seasoned and then browned on the stovetop, to add another layer of flavor. Next, it's layered with root vegetables in a slow cooker. The slow process of cooking the roast makes it fork-tender and your personal chef does most of the work.

Yield: 6 to 8 servings

Pot Roast:

1 (3½-pound) beef chuck roast
3 tablespoons Montreal steak
    seasoning
2 pounds carrots, peeled and sliced
3 pounds Yukon gold potatoes, cubed
1 large sweet onion, cut into wedges
4 garlic cloves, peeled and smashed
½ cup beef stock
½ cup Dr Pepper
3 tablespoons soy sauce
Salt and freshly ground black pepper
4 tablespoons salted butter, cubed

Gravy:

2 teaspoons Kitchen Bouquet
    Browning and Seasoning Sauce
3 tablespoons cornstarch dissolved
    in 3 tablespoons cold water, plus
    more if needed

Rub the chuck roast on all sides liberally with the steak seasoning. Heat a few drizzles of olive oil in a large skillet. Sear and brown the roast for 2 minutes on all sides.

Spray the inside of an oval 6-quart slow cooker with cooking spray.

Arrange the carrots in the bottom of the slow cooker. Center the seasoned roast on top. Arrange the potatoes around the edge of the roast. Arrange the onion wedges and smashed garlic over the roast.

In a small bowl, whisk together the beef stock, Dr Pepper, and soy sauce. Pour over the roast. Season lightly with salt and pepper, then dot the top with the butter.

Cook on HIGH for 4 hours or on LOW for 8 hours, or until the roast is fork-tender. Transfer the roast and vegetables to a platter and cover loosely with foil to keep warm while you make the gravy.

To make the gravy: Pour the drippings from the slow cooker into a saucepan. Add the Kitchen Bouquet sauce. Bring the drippings to a boil and slowly drizzle in the cornstarch slurry, whisking constantly. Add additional cornstarch slurry, if needed, until your desired consistency is reached.

Slice the roast, drizzle with gravy, and serve with the cooked vegetables on the side.

SWEET TOMATO-GLAZED MEAT LOAF

My family considers sweet tomato–glazed meat loaf ultimate comfort food. In the summer months when we gathered at my grandparents' farm in Virginia for family reunions, meat loaf was always on the menu. Aunt Joann's meat loaves were in hot demand and were usually among the first items to disappear.

I'm not certain whether it's the meat loaf or the anticipation of the leftover meat loaf sandwich that thrills me the most. Regardless, meat loaf is one dish in my repertoire that's here to stay. To make this free-form meat loaf, you must begin with a quality lean ground beef so the meat loaf will hold its shape while baking. It's topped with a sweet tomato glaze that takes the flavor over the top.

Yield: 8 servings

Sweet Tomato Glaze:

½ cup light brown sugar

⅔ cup ketchup

⅓ cup tomato basil marinara sauce

1½ teaspoons prepared yellow mustard

1 teaspoon barbecue seasoning

1 teaspoon cider vinegar

Meat Loaf:

1 medium-size sweet onion, diced

½ cup seeded and diced red bell pepper

½ cup seeded and diced green bell pepper

2 pounds lean ground beef (90/10)

1½ cups tomato basil marinara sauce

1 tablespoon prepared yellow mustard

1 tablespoon Worcestershire sauce

1 tablespoon barbecue seasoning

¼ teaspoon freshly ground black pepper

1 teaspoon salt

2 large eggs, beaten

¼ cup buttermilk

1 cup panko breadcrumbs

To make the glaze: Mix together the glaze ingredients until smooth. Set aside.

To make the meat loaf: Preheat the oven to 350°F. Line a rimmed baking sheet with aluminum foil sprayed liberally with cooking spray.

In a small skillet, heat a couple of drizzles of olive oil and sauté the onion and bell peppers until they begin to soften and turn translucent, 3 to 5 minutes. Season with salt and black pepper to taste. Set aside to cool slightly.

While the vegetables are cooking, mix together the ground beef, marinara sauce, yellow mustard, Worcestershire sauce, barbecue seasoning, black pepper, salt, eggs, buttermilk, and breadcrumbs. Add the cooled onion and bell peppers. Mix well.

In the bowl, roughly form the meat mixture into a loaf shape. Slide the loaf onto the center of the prepared baking sheet. Pat the meat loaf into an oblong loaf shape about 2½ inches thick. It's important to make the loaf proportional so it will cook evenly.

Pour half of the glaze over the meat loaf, covering the top and sides.

Place in the oven and bake for 55 minutes. Drizzle with the remaining glaze, return the meat loaf to the oven, and bake for an additional 10 to 15 minutes.

Allow the meat loaf to rest on the counter for at least 10 minutes before cutting and serving.

STUFFED TACO FRENCH BREAD LOAF

This Mexican-inspired stuffed torta falls into the category of "party food" at our house. It's filled with the festive taco flavors that we love. To make this party loaf, use one of those inexpensive fluffy loaves of French bread available in the bakery at your local market. It's perfect race day or game day food and it's meant for sharing with friends.

Yield: 12 servings

1 (18-inch) French bread loaf

1 small sweet onion, diced

½ medium-size red bell pepper, seeded and diced

1 small poblano pepper, seeded and diced

1 teaspoon salt

¼ teaspoon black pepper

3 garlic cloves, minced

1 pound lean ground beef

1 cup thick and chunky salsa (see Cook's Note)

8 ounces chive and onion cream cheese, softened

3 tablespoons taco seasoning

2 tablespoons sliced black olives

½ teaspoon ground cumin

2½ cups shredded Colby-Jack cheese, divided

24 green olives (optional; see Cook's Note)

Preheat the oven to 350°F. Line a standard baking sheet with a piece of aluminum foil double the length of the bread loaf. Spray the foil with cooking spray. Set aside.

Slice the French loaf in half. Hollow out the bread halves, leaving a ½-inch border. Place the bottom half onto the aluminum foil.

In a large skillet over medium-high heat, heat a couple of drizzles of olive oil. Add the onion, bell pepper, and poblano pepper. Season with salt and black pepper to taste. Cook until softened and beginning to brown. Add the garlic and cook for 1 minute.

Add the ground beef. Cook for 8 to 10 minutes, or until no pink remains. Drain any excess fat from the pan.

Add the salsa, cream cheese, taco seasoning, sliced black olives, and cumin. Continue to cook over low heat just until the cream cheese has melted. Remove from the heat and mix in ½ cup of the Colby-Jack cheese.

Sprinkle the bottom half of the French loaf with 1 cup of the cheese. Spread the filling evenly over the cheese from end to end, then sprinkle the filling with the remaining cup of cheese. Cover with aluminum foil.

Bake for 30 minutes. Rest for 5 minutes, then uncover and slice into 12 equal portions (see Cook's Note). Serve immediately.

COOK'S NOTES:
You may use mild, medium, or hot salsa depending on your taste.

To serve as a small-bite appetizer, after baking, slice the loaf the long way through the middle, from end to end, then evenly slice 11 times widthwise along the loaf, making 24 portions total. Secure each piece with a festive toothpick and a green olive.

SWEET OVEN BBQ SPARE RIBS

There's no reason you can't enjoy juicy fall-apart spare ribs year-round. When grilling isn't an option, you can still make flavorful spare ribs in the oven. These spare ribs are dry rubbed, then roasted in the oven low and slow. At the end of roasting, uncover and char, using the broiler setting, to give them the caramelized bark that makes them finger-lickin' good.

Yield: About 8 servings

4 pounds St. Louis–style spare ribs
    (2 slabs)

Dry Rub:
⅓ cup light brown sugar
2 tablespoons dark chili powder
1½ tablespoons seasoned salt
1 tablespoon ground cumin
1 tablespoon paprika
1 tablespoon granulated garlic
1 tablespoon granulated onion
1 tablespoon ancho chili powder
1 teaspoon lemon pepper
1 teaspoon freshly ground black
    pepper

1 cup prepared barbecue sauce, plus
    more for serving

Rinse and pat dry the ribs. Remove the membrane from the back of the ribs.

To make the dry rub: Mix together the dry rub ingredients and coat both slabs of ribs, generously rubbing into the meat on both sides.

Cover with plastic wrap and chill overnight.

To cook the ribs: Preheat the oven to 300°F. Line a jelly-roll pan or large, rimmed baking pan with aluminum foil. Lightly spray with cooking spray.

Remove the ribs from the plastic wrap and lay side by side in the prepared pan. Cover tightly with heavy-duty aluminum foil.

Bake for 4 hours, then test for tenderness. The ribs should be fork-tender. If not, continue to cook for an additional 30 minutes, then test again. When done, uncover and let cool slightly.

To char the sauce onto the ribs, increase the oven temperature to BROIL. Place the ribs on a clean broiler pan or rimmed baking sheet sprayed with cooking spray. Mop generously with your favorite barbecue sauce.

Broil the spare ribs for 3 to 5 minutes on each side, or until the sauce has charred. Turn and repeat on the other side. Do not walk away as you broil the ribs, as they char quickly.

Let rest for 10 minutes, divide and serve.

SLOW-COOKED PULLED PORK BBQ

North Carolinians love pulled pork barbecue. In eastern North Carolina you'll typically find pork with a spicy and tangy vinegar-based sauce, while barbecue fans in the western parts of the state prefer a sweet tomato-based sauce. It doesn't matter how you like to dress it—it all begins with succulent slow-cooked pulled pork. You don't need a smoker to make this tender dish in your slow cooker with no fuss at all.

Yield: 16 servings

1 (6-pound) pork butt
Vegetable oil

Dry Rub:
¼ cup light brown sugar
1 tablespoon garlic salt
1 tablespoon dark chili powder
1 tablespoon paprika
1 tablespoon ground cumin
2 teaspoons dry mustard
2 teaspoons onion powder
2 teaspoons lemon pepper
1 teaspoon freshly ground black
    pepper
1 teaspoon ground chipotle pepper

1 (12-ounce) can Dr Pepper
1 tablespoon liquid smoke

2 cups of your favorite prepared
    barbecue sauce, plus more for
    serving (optional)
Kaiser rolls, for serving (optional)
Creamy Coleslaw (page 123), for
    serving (optional)

Rinse and pat dry the pork butt. Rub lightly with vegetable oil.

To make the dry rub: Mix together the dry rub ingredients and rub generously on all sides of the pork butt. Place on a platter and cover with plastic wrap. Chill overnight.

To cook the pork: Spray the bottom and sides of an oval 6-quart slow cooker with cooking spray.

In a small bowl, mix together the Dr Pepper and liquid smoke and pour into the bottom of the prepared slow cooker. Center the pork butt in the slow cooker and cover tightly. Cook on LOW for 9 to 10 hours.

After the pork has cooked, uncover and drain and discard the jus. Use two forks to shred the pork, removing any visible fat.

Return the pulled pork to the slow cooker and drizzle with 2 cups of barbecue sauce. Do not stir. Cook on HIGH for 45 minutes, or just until the sauce has cooked through the pork.

Serve on toasted kaiser rolls with coleslaw and the remaining cup of barbecue sauce on the side, if desired.

PINEAPPLE-GLAZED JAMAICAN JERK PORK TENDERLOIN

This Jamaican jerk–seasoned pork tenderloin has an enticing
sweet-and-spicy flavor combination. Serve it on a bed of fluffy rice pilaf
and you can enjoy a taste of the islands without a passport.

Yield: About 10 (4-ounce) servings

2 (1½-pound) pork tenderloin

¼ cup minced sweet onion

2 tablespoons olive oil

2 tablespoons teriyaki sauce

2 tablespoons Jamaican jerk
    seasoning, divided (see
    Cook's Note)

1 tablespoon freshly squeezed lime
    juice

1 teaspoon garlic salt

½ teaspoon freshly ground black
    pepper

1 (12-ounce) jar pineapple preserves

1 tablespoon cider vinegar

1 teaspoon crushed red pepper flakes

Rinse and pat dry the pork tenderloin.

In a small bowl, mix together the onion, olive oil, teriyaki sauce,
1½ tablespoons of the Jamaican Jerk seasoning, lime juice, garlic salt,
and black pepper. Rub over the pork tenderloin. Place in a reusable
plastic bag. Chill for at least 4 hours or overnight.

Preheat the oven to 375°F. Heat a few drizzles of olive oil on an oven-
safe grill pan. Remove the tenderloin from the plastic bag, shaking
off any excess marinade. Place on the hot grill pan. Sprinkle with the
remaining 1½ teaspoons of Jamaican jerk seasoning on all sides. Sear
the tenderloin for 2 minutes on each side over high heat, then transfer
the pan to the oven.

Mix together the pineapple preserves, vinegar, and red pepper flakes.
Set aside.

Roast the tenderloin for 25 minutes, then increase the oven
temperature to 425°F. Begin to baste with the pineapple mixture.
Continue to roast for 4 minutes, then turn and repeat for a total of 4 to
6 minutes on each side. Adjust the timing depending on the thickness
of the pork.

Remove from the oven and place on a cutting board to rest *un*covered
for 10 minutes.

Pour the pan juices into the remaining pineapple mixture and warm on
the stovetop or in the microwave. Slice the tenderloin and arrange on
a platter. Serve drizzled with the pineapple glaze.

COOK'S NOTE:
Each brand of Jerk seasoning features different amounts of
ingredients, such as salt and spice. Adjust the amount of seasoning,
using more or less based on your preferred brand.

BAKED RIGATONI WITH ITALIAN SAUSAGE AND PEPPERONI

This rigatoni bake is one of those make-ahead, Italian-inspired meals that always hits the spot. The Italian sausage gives the sauce such a rich, bold flavor. If you prefer, this dish could be made with all beef or a combination of beef and sausage. It's also quite tasty with ground chicken or turkey. I like to assemble this dish a day in advance and tuck it away in the fridge. The next day it's ready to pop in the oven to bake with no fuss and the flavor becomes even more robust.

Yield: 12 servings

1 pound rigatoni

1 medium-size onion, diced

3 garlic cloves, minced

2 pounds spicy or mild Italian sausage

2 teaspoons dried Italian seasoning

1 teaspoon salt

½ teaspoon freshly ground black pepper

½ teaspoon red pepper flakes

2 (24-ounce) jars marinara sauce

4 ounces chive and onion cream cheese, softened

½ cup mini pepperoni

¼ cup grated Parmesan cheese

1 cup shredded fontina cheese

2 cups shredded mozzarella cheese, divided

Preheat the oven to 350°F. Spray a 9 × 13-inch baking dish with cooking spray. Set aside.

Cook the rigatoni in salted water per the instructions on the package. Drain well.

In a large skillet, heat a couple of drizzles of olive oil. Add the onion to the pan. Cook for 2 to 3 minutes, or until softened and translucent. Add the garlic and continue to cook for 1 additional minute.

Add the Italian sausage to the pan. Cook over medium-high heat for 8 minutes, or until no pink remains. Drain all excess fat from the pan.

Remove from the heat. Add the Italian seasoning, salt, black pepper, red pepper flakes, marinara sauce, cream cheese, mini pepperoni, and Parmesan cheese. Mix until combined and the cream cheese has melted.

Add the fontina cheese and 1 cup of the mozzarella cheese. Mix well.

Pour into the prepared baking dish and sprinkle with the remaining cup of mozzarella cheese.

Bake for 35 to 40 minutes, or until the mozzarella cheese is lightly browned and the edges are bubbly.

Let rest on the counter for 10 minutes before serving.

CHEESY BACON RANCH CHICKEN SPAGHETTI

Baked pasta casseroles like this one are a go-to favorite of mine because they can be assembled in advance and popped into the oven when it's mealtime. The creamy ranch sauce is so delicious, no one will ever believe you whipped it up using your blender.

Yield: 12 servings

¾ pound thin spaghetti

3 cups roughly chopped roasted chicken

8 slices bacon, cooked and crumbled

1 (14-ounce) can low-sodium chicken stock

1 (10¾-ounce) can cream of celery soup

8 ounces chive and onion cream cheese, softened

8 ounces sour cream

½ cup real mayonnaise

1 (0.4-ounce) packet dried buttermilk ranch dressing mix

1½ tablespoons chopped fresh chives, divided

1 teaspoon garlic powder

¼ teaspoon freshly ground black pepper

3 cups shredded sharp cheddar cheese, divided

Preheat the oven to 350°F. Spray a 9 × 13-inch baking dish with cooking spray. Set aside.

Cook the spaghetti in salted water per the package instructions until al dente. Drain well. Place in a large mixing bowl.

Add the chicken and all 2 tablespoons of the bacon crumbles to the bowl, reserving the remaining bacon crumbles for garnish.

In a stand blender, combine the chicken stock, celery soup, cream cheese, sour cream, mayonnaise, ranch dressing, 1 tablespoon of the chives, and the garlic powder and pepper. Blend until smooth and fully combined.

Pour the blended mixture over the spaghetti. Add 1 cup of the cheddar cheese. Mix well.

Pour half of the spaghetti mixture into the prepared baking dish. Sprinkle with 1 cup of the cheddar cheese. Repeat with the remaining spaghetti, topping with the remaining cup of cheddar cheese.

Bake for 35 to 40 minutes, or until golden and bubbly. Let rest on the counter for 5 minutes. Garnish with the reserved bacon crumbles and remaining chives just before serving.

PHILLY CHEESESTEAK PASTA BAKE

The only way to describe this cheese-laden cheesesteak pasta bake is "ooey and gooey."
This dish takes everything you love about a cheesesteak sub and tosses it with
corkscrew pasta. Voilà, dinner is served.

Yield: 8 servings

12 ounces dry corkscrew pasta, such
as cavatappi

1½ pounds thinly sliced sirloin steak

3 teaspoons Montreal steak
seasoning, divided

1 medium-size onion, diced

1 medium-size green bell pepper,
seeded and diced

8 ounces baby portobello mushrooms

Salt and freshly ground black pepper

3 garlic cloves, minced

1 pound deli white American cheese,
cubed

2½ cups half-and-half

4 ounces chive and onion cream
cheese, softened

2 teaspoons dried Italian seasoning

2 cups shredded mozzarella cheese,
divided

2 tablespoons salted butter, melted

½ cup panko breadcrumbs

3 tablespoons grated Parmesan
cheese

Preheat the oven to 350°F. Spray a 9 × 13-inch baking dish with
cooking spray. Set aside.

Cook the pasta in salted water per the package instructions until al
dente. Drain well.

In a large skillet, heat a few drizzles of olive oil. Season the steak with
1 teaspoon of the steak seasoning and add to the pan. Cook, browning
on both sides, until medium rare, about 2 minutes, then remove from
the pan.

Add the onion, bell pepper, and mushrooms to the pan, plus additional
olive oil, if needed. Sauté over medium-high heat for 5 to 7 minutes,
or until golden and beginning to brown. Season with salt and black
pepper to taste. Add the garlic and cook until fragrant, around
1 minute.

Meanwhile, in a separate pot, combine the American cheese and
half-and-half over medium-high heat. Simmer, stirring occasionally,
until the cheese has melted. Add the cream cheese and continue
to cook for another 1 to 2 minutes, or until the cream cheese is fully
incorporated into the cheese sauce.

Season the sauce with the remaining 2 teaspoons of steak seasoning
and the Italian seasoning. Remove from the heat and add 1 cup of the
mozzarella cheese. Mix well.

Pour the sauce over the cooked pasta and stir in the cooked steak
and vegetables. Mix until fully combined, then pour into the prepared
baking dish. Top with the remaining cup of mozzarella cheese.

In a small bowl, toss together the melted butter, breadcrumbs, and
Parmesan cheese. Sprinkle on top of the pasta mixture.

Bake for 30 to 35 minutes, or until golden and bubbly. Serve
immediately.

Decadent Desserts

Americans love sweets and the South is famous for so many classics. We also love history and that's why so many of our desserts come with a side of nostalgia. During my childhood, family reunions were a regular summertime event for my dad's extremely large family. Long tables were set up outside under the shade trees and filled with all of the best of Southern cuisine. The magnificent desserts were usually arranged separately, inside the main house, to protect the cream cheese frostings, whipped cream-laden pies, and cheesecakes from the summer heat.

One of the most sought-after desserts was Granma Minnie's famous blueberry icebox pie, for which the recipe was known to her alone. Most old-school cooks used no written recipes, so recipes were shared literally by mouth. I vividly remember visiting with her one afternoon as she told me how to re-create her icebox pie. While I dearly wish I had it in her own handwriting now that she is no longer with us, I can continue to keep the tradition alive by making her pie for my own family. I'll treasure the memory of that afternoon with her for a lifetime and, in turn, accept the honor of passing her recipe on to the next generation. It's true: The best things in life are free, and in this case, they're also sweet.

CARROT CAKE WITH A COCONUT-PECAN CREAM CHEESE FROSTING

This spectacular carrot cake recipe is from my mom's recipe file. It differs from many carrot cakes in that there are no raisins or nuts in the cake layers themselves. However, the cream cheese frosting is laced with both fresh coconut and toasted pecans. My mom insists the secret to this cake is shredding the carrots finely by hand using a box grater, and has made it precisely that way for decades. The coconut- and pecan-laden cream cheese frosting adds the crowning touch to this sweet taste of nostalgia from my childhood.

Yield: 1 (8-inch) triple-layer or 1 (9-inch) double-layer cake

Cake:

2 cups self-rising flour, plus more for pans

2 cups granulated sugar

2 teaspoons ground cinnamon

1 teaspoon salt

¼ teaspoon ground nutmeg

¼ teaspoon ground ginger

4 large eggs

1¼ cups vegetable oil

2 teaspoons pure vanilla extract

3 cups finely grated fresh carrot

1 cup sweetened shredded coconut

Frosting:

2 cups chopped pecans, toasted

2 (8-ounce) packages cream cheese, softened

1 cup (2 stick, or 8 ounces) salted butter, at room temperature

2 teaspoons pure vanilla extract

2 (16-ounce) boxes powdered sugar

1 (6-ounce) package frozen coconut, thawed and patted dry (if you can't find frozen coconut, you can use sweetened shredded coconut in its place)

To make the cake: Preheat the oven to 325°F. Butter and flour three 8-inch or two 9-inch round cake pans. Set aside.

Sift together the flour, sugar, cinnamon, salt, nutmeg, and ginger.

Whisk together the eggs, oil, and vanilla. Add to the dry ingredients, using a large, nonstick spatula. Mix by hand until fully moistened. Add the carrot and shredded coconut. Mix well.

Divide the batter evenly among the prepared pans. Bounce the pans on the counter to remove any trapped air bubbles.

Bake for 35 to 40 minutes, or until a toothpick inserted into the center comes back clean. Remove from the oven and let cool completely in the pans on a cooling rack.

To make the frosting: While the cake layers cool, increase the oven temperature to 350°F. Spread the pecans in a single layer on a baking sheet. Toast for 6 to 8 minutes. Let cool completely.

Using an electric mixer, cream together the cream cheese, butter, and vanilla. Beat for 2 to 3 minutes, or until light and fluffy. Gradually add the powdered sugar. After all the powdered sugar has been added, increase the speed of the mixer and beat for 2 minutes.

Fold in the thawed coconut and toasted pecans by hand. Mix well.

Frost between the layers, and on the sides and top of the cake. Decorate as desired. Store chilled.

LEMON SOUR CREAM POUND CAKE

Pound cakes in every flavor are a sought-after confection. They were originally developed using a pound of butter, a pound of flour, a pound of sugar, and a pound of eggs. Through the years, bakers have modified the ingredients and added other flavorings to suit their own taste.

This cake is drizzled with a lemony glaze in the same style that my mother-in-law glazes her cakes and it's delightful served as is or topped with fresh berries and a dollop of fresh whipped cream. It makes the perfect sweet ending to any meal.

Yield: 1 (10-inch) tube pan cake

Cake:

Unsalted butter, for pan

3 cups all-purpose flour, plus more
    for pan

1 (3.4-ounce) package instant lemon
    pudding

½ teaspoon salt

¼ teaspoon baking soda

1½ cups (3 sticks, or 12 ounces) salted
    butter, at room temperature

2¾ cups granulated sugar

2 teaspoons pure vanilla extract

6 large eggs

8 ounces sour cream

2 tablespoons lemon zest

Glaze:

1½ cups powdered sugar

2 tablespoons freshly squeezed lemon
    juice, plus more if needed, to thin

1 tablespoon salted butter, melted

To make the cake: Preheat the oven to 325°F. Butter and flour a standard 10-inch tube pan. Set aside.

Sift together the flour, lemon pudding mix, salt, and baking soda.

Cream together the butter, granulated sugar, and vanilla. Beat for 2 to 3 minutes, or until light and pale yellow in color. Add the eggs, one at a time, beating well after each addition, stopping and scraping the sides of the bowl as needed.

Reduce the speed of the mixer and add the sifted dry ingredients alternately with the sour cream. Mix until fully combined. Stir in the fresh lemon zest by hand.

Pour into the prepared tube pan and place in the oven.

Bake, placing a piece of aluminum foil on top to prevent overbrowning, if needed, for 1 hour 20 minutes to 1 hour 30 minutes, or until a toothpick inserted into the center comes back clean.

Remove from the oven and let cool in the pan on a cooling rack for 15 minutes, then remove from the pan and let cool completely.

To make the glaze: In a medium-size mixing bowl, mix together the powdered sugar, lemon juice, and butter. Drizzle over the cooled cake.

FRENCH VANILLA CAKE WITH FRESH STRAWBERRY CREAM CHEESE FROSTING

This cake is as pretty as it is tasty. It's a celebration of the flavor combination of strawberries and cream otherwise known as "angel food" in my kitchen. This cake is so decadent, it deserves to be the centerpiece of your summertime desserts.

Yield: 1 (8- or 9-inch) double-layer cake

Cake:

3 cups cake flour, plus more for pan (optional)

1 tablespoon baking powder

½ teaspoon salt

1 cup (2 sticks, or 8 ounces) salted butter, at room temperature

2 cups granulated sugar

2 teaspoons vanilla bean paste, or 1 tablespoon pure vanilla extract

3 large eggs

3 large egg whites

1½ cups whole buttermilk

Fresh Strawberry Cream Cheese Frosting:

1 cup (2 sticks, or 8 ounces) salted butter, at room temperature

2 (8-ounce) packages cream cheese, softened

1 teaspoon pure vanilla extract

½ teaspoon pure almond extract

2 (16-ounce) boxes powdered sugar, plus more as needed

1 cup finely diced fresh strawberries

2–3 drops red food coloring

Heavy cream or strawberry purée (see Cook's Note), to thin if needed

Whole strawberries, for garnish

To make the cake: Preheat the oven to 350°F. Grease and flour two 8- or 9-inch cake pans or spray with cooking spray. Set aside.

Sift together the flour, baking powder, and salt.

In the bowl of a stand mixer, cream together the butter, granulated sugar, and vanilla bean paste. Beat for 5 minutes, or until creamy and pale yellow in color.

Add the whole eggs, one at a time, beating well after each addition. Next, add all the egg whites. Continue to beat on medium-high speed for 2 minutes, or until fluffy.

Reduce the speed of the mixer and add the sifted dry ingredients alternately with the buttermilk, stopping and scraping the beater and sides of the bowl periodically so all the ingredients fully combine. After all the ingredients have been added, increase the mixer speed and beat for 1 minute longer.

Divide the batter between the prepared pans. Bounce each pan on the counter a few times to settle the batter and remove any air bubbles.

Bake for 25 minutes, or until a toothpick inserted into the center comes back clean and the top is golden. Remove from the oven and let cool completely on a cooling rack.

To make the frosting: Cream together the butter, cream cheese, and vanilla and almond extracts. Beat with an electric mixer for 3 minutes, or until completely smooth and fluffy.

Reduce the speed of the mixer and gradually add the powdered sugar, mixing until fully moistened.

continued on next page

Add the diced strawberries and 2 to 3 drops of red food coloring and continue to whip until fully combined. Some strawberry chunks will remain. To thicken the frosting, add additional powdered sugar as needed; to thin the frosting, add cream or purée 1 tablespoon at a time until your desired consistency is reached. You will probably have frosting left over, as this makes about 6 cups' worth.

Spread the frosting between the layers and on the top and sides of the cake. Garnish with additional fresh strawberries, if desired. Store chilled.

COOK'S NOTE:
In place of heavy cream, you may use strawberry purée to thin the frosting, if desired.

WHITE CHOCOLATE MARSHMALLOW FRUIT DIP

Creamy white chocolate adds subtle undertones to this decadent fruit dip, and its mild flavor pairs well with any type of fruit. Prepare this in advance and serve it with seasonal fresh fruit.

Yield: About 2 cups dip

½ cup white chocolate chips
3 tablespoons heavy cream
8 ounces cream cheese, softened
½ cup powdered sugar
1 teaspoon pure vanilla extract
7 ounces marshmallow fluff
Assorted fresh fruit, for dipping

In a small, microwave-safe bowl, combine the white chocolate chips and cream and melt at 50 percent power in 20-second increments, stopping to stir each time, until smooth. Set aside to cool slightly.

In a medium-size mixing bowl, use an electric mixer on medium-high speed to cream together the cream cheese, powdered sugar, and vanilla until fluffy. Add the melted white chocolate mixture, continuing to beat until fully blended.

Reduce the speed of the mixer to medium and add the marshmallow fluff. Mix until just combined.

Cover and chill until serving. Serve with fresh fruit.

MISSISSIPPI MUD BROWNIES

The origin of the whimsical name "Mississippi mud" is always a source of debate with no definitive explanation. One thing we can all agree on is these rich brownies are truly the tastiest "mud" you'll ever eat, topped with gooey marshmallows and toasted pecans then drizzled with a silky chocolate ganache. One heavenly bite and you may think you hear angels singing.

Yield: 24 brownies

1½ cups chopped pecans
1 cup all-purpose flour
1¾ cups granulated sugar
¼ cup packed light brown sugar
½ teaspoon salt
¾ cup (1½ sticks, or 6 ounces) salted butter
4 ounces unsweetened chocolate, chopped
1 teaspoon espresso powder
½ teaspoon pure vanilla extract
4 large eggs
1 (10-ounce) bag miniature marshmallows
1 cup semisweet chocolate chips
⅓ cup heavy cream

Preheat the oven to 350°F. Spray a 9 × 13-inch baking dish liberally with cooking spray. Set aside.

Spread the chopped pecans in a single layer on a baking sheet. Place in the oven and toast for 6 to 8 minutes. Set aside to cool completely.

In a medium-size mixing bowl, sift together the flour, granulated sugar, brown sugar, and salt.

In a microwave-safe bowl, combine the butter and chocolate and melt in 20-second increments, stopping to stir each time, until smooth.

Add the espresso powder and vanilla to the melted chocolate mixture, stirring until the espresso has dissolved.

Using an electric mixer, gradually beat the chocolate mixture into the dry ingredients. Add the eggs and beat for 1 minute. Pour into the prepared pan.

Bake for 28 to 30 minutes, or until a toothpick inserted into the center shows moist crumbs. *Do not overbake.*

Remove from the oven and immediately pour the marshmallows on top and spread. Sprinkle with half of the toasted pecans.

In a microwave-safe bowl, combine the chocolate chips and cream and melt in 20-second increments, until smooth. Drizzle over the top of the brownies.

Let cool to room temperature, then cut and serve.

CHOCOLATE CHIP TOFFEE POTATO CHIP COOKIES

These crazy delicious sweet and salty cookies are a twist on classic chocolate chip cookies. The ever-popular flavor combination is sure to satisfy your need for salty-sweet munching.

Yield: 32 (3-inch) cookies

2¼ cups all-purpose flour

1 teaspoon baking powder

¾ teaspoon salt

½ teaspoon baking soda

1 cup (2 sticks, or 8 ounces) unsalted butter, at room temperature

¾ cup light brown sugar

¾ cup granulated sugar

2 teaspoons pure vanilla extract

2 large eggs

3 cups crushed potato chips with ridges

1 (12-ounce) package milk chocolate chips

½ cup toffee bits

Sift together the flour, baking powder, salt, and baking soda. Set aside.

In the bowl of a stand mixer, cream together the butter, brown sugar, granulated sugar, and vanilla. Add the eggs one at a time, beating well after each addition.

While the mixer is running, gradually add the sifted dry ingredients to the bowl. After all have been added, beat just until all of the ingredients are incorporated, stopping and scraping the sides of the bowl periodically.

Use a large, nonstick spatula to mix the crushed potato chips, chocolate chips, and toffee bits into the dough. Mix until the ingredients are evenly distributed.

Chill for 30 minutes to 1 hour.

To bake, preheat the oven to 350°F. Line a baking sheet with parchment paper. One batch at a time, use a 2-ounce ice-cream scoop or a tablespoon to drop the dough at least 2 inches apart onto the pan, to allow room for spreading.

Bake for 14 to 16 minutes, or until lightly golden. Keep the cookie dough chilled between batches.

Remove from the oven and let the baked cookies cool on the pan for 5 minutes, then transfer to a cooling rack to cool completely.

LOADED MONSTER COOKIE BARS

To the delight of my children, I love cookies and milk as much as they do. This recipe allows you to bake the entire cookie dough batch in one fell swoop. Serve these goodies slightly warm so you can fully savor the gooey peanut butter and chocolate chips nestled inside the dough. Milk isn't optional.

Yield: 30 cookie bars

2 cups all-purpose flour

1 teaspoon salt

1 teaspoon baking powder

½ teaspoon baking soda

1 cup (2 sticks, or 8 ounces) unsalted
  butter, at room temperature

1 cup granulated sugar

1 cup light brown sugar

⅔ cup peanut butter

2 teaspoons pure vanilla extract

2 large eggs

1½ cups quick-cooking oatmeal

1 cup roughly chopped peanuts

1 cup milk chocolate chips

1 cup peanut butter chips

1½ cups M&M's candies

Preheat the oven to 350°F. Liberally spray a metal nonstick 9 × 13-inch baking pan with cooking spray. Set aside.

Sift together the all-purpose flour, salt, baking powder, and baking soda. Set aside.

In the bowl of a stand mixer, cream together the butter, granulated sugar, brown sugar, peanut butter, and vanilla. Beat for 2 minutes, or until fluffy and light beige in color. Add the eggs one at a time, beating well after each addition.

Reduce the speed of the mixer and gradually add the sifted dry ingredients, stopping and scraping the sides periodically. After all the flour has been added, beat for 1 minute.

By hand, mix in the oats, peanuts, milk chocolate chips, peanut butter chips, and M&M's. Mix until the ingredients are evenly distributed. The batter will be stiff.

Spread the cookie dough evenly in the prepared pan. Bake for 30 minutes, or until golden and a toothpick inserted into the center comes back clean.

Remove from the oven and let cool in the pan on a cooling rack. Cut into squares and serve.

EASY PIECRUST

If you just say the phrase *homemade piecrust*, people start turning all shades of pale and I'm convinced they're going to break out in hives. It evokes such a strong reaction because most people think it's an unreachable goal and that they're simply impossible to make. I believe anyone can learn the technique for making piecrusts from scratch. The best part is, it doesn't take a long list of fancy ingredients, as you'll find most of the items in your pantry. That said, there are a few things to remember to guarantee your piecrust-making success (see sidebar).

Yield: 2 (9- to 10-inch) piecrusts

3 cups all-purpose flour, plus more for dusting

1 teaspoon salt

¾ cup (1½ sticks, or 6 ounces) unsalted cold butter, cubed

¼ cup cold butter-flavored shortening, cubed

1 teaspoon cold white distilled vinegar

⅓ to ½ cup ice water

Place the flour and salt in the bowl of a food processor fitted with a steel blade (see Cook's Note). Pulse a few times to combine.

Add the butter and shortening. Pulse eight to ten times, or until the butter is the size of peas.

Drizzle the vinegar and cold water 1 tablespoon at a time through the tube of the food processor. Continue to pulse, adding cold water until the dough forms a ball.

Remove from the food processor and divide in half. Gently shape each portion into a disk and wrap with plastic wrap. Refrigerate for at least 30 minutes.

When ready to make a pie, on a lightly floured nonstick surface, roll out one disk of dough. Place a piece of waxed paper on top to prevent the dough from sticking to the rolling pin. Think like a clock: Roll away from you to 12 o'clock, letting up on pressure as you reach the edge so it won't be too thin. Then roll back toward you to 6 o'clock. Then 3 and 9 o'clock. Turn the dough to prevent it from sticking on the counter. Repeat until the desired size is reached.

Drape the crust over the rolling pin and transfer to your pie dish. Fit firmly into the dish, and fold and flute the edges or press with the tines of a fork. Fill or blind bake.

COOK'S NOTES:
To make a sweeter piecrust, add 1 tablespoon of granulated sugar to the dry ingredients, then proceed with the recipe as written.

Unflavored shortening may be used in place of butter-flavored shortening, if desired.

Piecrust-Making Tips

- When making homemade piecrust dough, everything has to be cold—the only exception being the flour. The water, the butter, the shortening, and the vinegar. Everything.

- Handle the dough as little as possible. Unlike with bread dough, you don't want the gluten in the flour to activate and make the dough tough. No kneading allowed.

- Enter vinegar. Vinegar actually interrupts the formation of the gluten in the dough and makes for a more tender crust. Vodka, substituted in the same amount, will work as well.

- The piecrust debate seems to always gravitate to the type of fat used in the dough. The discussion centers on butter versus shortening and people have strong opinions both ways. Butter is my preferred flavor, but when it comes to crusts, you need shortening to give it a flaky texture. An all-butter crust is a bit more finicky, making it a bit harder to work with as well. Some bakers use all butter; some prefer all shortening or lard; and others, like myself, prefer to go the middle of the road and use part butter and part butter-flavored shortening. It always works.

- A food processor is so handy to make the dough, but if you don't have one, use the tools God gave you. Rub the butter or shortening into the dough using your hands or a pastry cutter. Use the tips of your fingers only and not the palm, which is a warmer part of your hand. Remember, everything must stay cold.

- After making the dough, divide it in half, shape into a disk, then wrap with plastic wrap. You can freeze the dough at this point, if you're making it in advance, or refrigerate for 30 minutes, if using immediately.

- To blind bake the crust, fit it into a pie dish. Fold the edges, then flute. Prick the bottom with a fork and fit with parchment or aluminum foil before filling with pie weights or beans. Bake at 425°F for 15 minutes, or until golden, then remove the liner and weights and fill with your favorite fillings.

BLACK-BOTTOMED PEANUT BUTTER PIE

You can find variations of peanut butter pie all throughout the South. It's particularly loved in the hot summer months, since the filling requires no baking at all. This can be made several days in advance, then topped with whipped cream, peanut butter cups, and warm chocolate ganache just before serving. It's guaranteed to thrill the chocolate peanut butter fans at your dessert table.

Yield: 1 (10-inch) pie

Crust:

2¼ cups crushed chocolate graham cracker crumbs

¼ cup granulated sugar

½ cup (1 stick, or 4 ounces) tablespoons salted butter, melted

To make the crust: Preheat the oven to 350°F. Lightly spray a 10-inch deep-dish pie dish with cooking spray. Set aside.

In a small mixing bowl, mix together the graham cracker crumbs, granulated sugar, and butter. The mixture should hold together when pressed between two fingers. Press firmly onto the bottom and up the sides of the prepared pie dish.

Bake for 15 minutes, or until set. Remove from the oven and let cool completely.

Filling:

2 (8-ounce) packages cream cheese, softened

1 cup smooth peanut butter

1 cup powdered sugar

2 teaspoons pure vanilla extract

2 (8-ounce) containers frozen whipped topping, thawed

To make the filling: In a medium-size mixing bowl, cream together the cream cheese, peanut butter, powdered sugar, and vanilla. Fold in half of the whipped topping by hand.

Spread the filling into the cooled piecrust. Top with the remaining whipped cream.

Topping:

1 (11-ounce) bag mini peanut butter cups, unwrapped and cubed

¼ cup semisweet chocolate chips

2 tablespoons heavy cream

¼ cup chopped peanuts

To top: Arrange the cubed peanut butter cups on top of the whipped cream.

In a microwave-safe bowl, combine the chocolate chips and cream and melt in 20-second increments, stopping to stir each time, until completely smooth.

Drizzle the chocolate mixture over the peanut butter cups and sprinkle with the chopped peanuts. This may be done just before serving, if desired. Chill for at least 4 hours to set.

GRANMA'S FAMOUS BLUEBERRY ICEBOX PIE

This icebox pie is my Granma Minnie's recipe. She was an old-school cook who raised and fed 13 children without a single written recipe. I recall sitting with her one afternoon at her table as she verbally told me how to re-create this goodie and now I make it for my own family. It boasts a creamy no-bake cheesecake filling and it's topped with a brilliantly vibrant blueberry pie filling, making it a true feast for the eyes. There's no need for words—just step aside and hand me a fork.

Yield: 1 (9-inch) pie

Crust:

2 cups graham cracker crumbs

⅓ cup salted butter, melted

¼ cup sliced almonds, roughly chopped

¼ cup granulated sugar

To make the crust: Preheat the oven to 350°F. Lightly spray a 9-inch pie dish with cooking spray. Set aside.

In a medium-size mixing bowl, toss together the graham cracker crumbs, butter, almonds, and granulated sugar. Press firmly onto the bottom and sides of the prepared pie dish.

Bake for 12 to 15 minutes, or until set and beginning to brown. Remove from the oven and let cool completely.

Cream Cheese Filling:

2 (8-ounce) packages cream cheese, softened

1 (2.6-ounce) box Dream Whip (see Cook's Note)

1 cup heavy cream

1 cup powdered sugar

½ teaspoon pure vanilla extract

½ teaspoon pure almond extract

1 (18-ounce) can premium blueberry pie filling

1 cup sweetened fresh whipped cream (optional)

To make the filling: In a medium-size mixing bowl, use an electric mixer to mix the cream cheese, Dream Whip, cream, powdered sugar, and vanilla and almond extracts. Beat for 2 minutes, or until fluffy and smooth.

Spread evenly into the cooled crust. Spread the blueberry pie filling on top.

Refrigerate for at least 4 hours, preferably overnight, before serving.

COOK'S NOTE:
Dream Whip is a brand of dried whipped topping mix. One 2.6 ounce box contains two envelopes. Use both envelopes for this icebox pie.

CHESS PIE

Classic chess pie has been a source of great conversation with many theories circulating
as to how it earned its name. Origin aside, it's a simple pie that's made by combining common
ingredients, such as flour, sugar, butter, and eggs. It often has slight flavor variations, with
some recipes including cornmeal and others not, depending on the cook's preference.
I prefer the texture that cornmeal gives to the filling and I include it in this recipe.
While it is simple to make, there's nothing mediocre about this luscious pie.

Yield: 1 (9-inch) pie

1 (9-inch) deep-dish piecrust,
    refrigerated, frozen, or
    homemade, such as ½ recipe
    Easy Piecrust (page 176)
1¾ cups granulated sugar
⅓ cup whole milk
4 tablespoons salted butter, melted
2 tablespoons plain cornmeal
1 tablespoon all-purpose flour
1 tablespoon white distilled vinegar
2 teaspoons pure vanilla extract
½ teaspoon salt
4 large eggs, beaten

Preheat the oven to 425°F. Fit the crust into a 9-inch pie dish and line
with parchment paper. Fill with beans or pie weights.

Bake for 10 minutes, then remove the parchment and weights and
bake for an additional 2 minutes. Remove from the oven and let cool
slightly. Lower the oven temperature to 350°F.

In a medium-size mixing bowl, whisk together the sugar, milk, butter,
cornmeal, flour, vinegar, vanilla, and salt. Add the eggs. Mix until fully
combined, then pour into the parbaked crust.

Bake for 45 to 55 minutes, checking at 20 minutes and covering the
edges of the crust with aluminum foil to prevent overbrowning.

Remove from the oven and let cool completely before cutting into
pieces for serving.

UNCLE SAM'S OLD-FASHIONED PEACH COBBLER

This peach cobbler is how my Uncle Sam was taught to make it by his mama and my Granma Vera. Uncle Sam is a larger-than-life character who is a bluegrass picker and expert on Appalachian history, which he once taught at the college level. He's retired now but keeps the road hot traveling to bluegrass festivals where he both judges and competes. I'm sure he would agree this must be topped with a scoop or two of vanilla ice cream, making it a true nostalgic treat.

Yield: 8 servings

½ cup (1 stick, or 4 ounces) unsalted butter
1 cup self-rising flour
1 cup granulated sugar
1 cup whole milk
1 large egg
1 quart sliced canned peaches, drained

Preheat the oven to 350°F. Place the butter in a 10-inch cast-iron skillet and into the oven to melt while it preheats.

Meanwhile, in small mixing bowl, whisk together the flour, sugar, milk, and egg.

Remove the skillet from the oven and swirl to coat the bottom and sides. Pour the batter evenly into the hot skillet over the melted butter.

Using a tablespoon, drop the peaches over the batter.

Place back in the oven and bake for 30 to 35 minutes, or until golden and puffy.

Serve warm with vanilla ice cream.

CHERRY PIE FLUFF

Vintage no-bake desserts, such as this cherry pie fluff, are especially appetizing
during warm weather. This is perfect for when you need a sweet fix in a snap, whipping
up in 5 minutes flat. It is oh-so-pretty when served in parfait glasses.

Yield: 10 servings

1 cup chopped pecans or walnuts

1 (20-ounce) can premium cherry pie
   filling

1 (20-ounce) can crushed pineapple,
   drained

1 (14-ounce) can sweetened
   condensed milk

½ teaspoon pure almond extract

4 cups fresh sweetened whipped
   cream

Preheat the oven to 350°F. Spread the nuts in a single layer on a
baking sheet. Toast for 6 to 8 minutes, or until lightly golden, then set
aside to cool completely.

In a medium-size mixing bowl, mix together the cherry pie filling,
crushed pineapple, sweetened condensed milk, and almond extract.

Fold in the whipped cream and toasted nuts by hand, reserving ½ cup
of the whipped cream and 1 tablespoon of the nuts.

Top with whipped cream and sprinkle the nuts on top. Chill thoroughly
for at least 4 hours before serving.

WHITE CHOCOLATE RASPBERRY CREAM TART

There are few dessert combinations more decadent than berries and cream. This simple tart starts with a buttery puff pastry crust that's topped with a fluffy filling of white chocolate cream and fresh raspberries. Garnish with a sprinkle of freshly grated white chocolate to finish it off just before serving.

Yield: 8 servings

½ (17.3 ounce) package puff pastry (1 sheet)

1 large egg, beaten

1 cup white chocolate chips

2½ cups heavy cream, divided

⅔ cup powdered sugar

8 ounces cream cheese, softened

1 teaspoon pure vanilla extract

¼ teaspoon pure almond extract

12 ounces fresh raspberries, rinsed and dried

2 tablespoons grated white chocolate

Preheat the oven to 400°F. Thaw the puff pastry per the package instructions.

Lightly spray a 14 × 5-inch fluted tart pan with a removable bottom with cooking spray. Set aside

On a floured nonstick surface, roll the puff pastry into roughly a 16 × 6-inch rectangle. Fit firmly into the tart pan and trim the edges.

Prick the bottom of the crust with a fork, then brush with the egg wash. Line with parchment paper and fill with pie weights or beans. Bake for 20 minutes, or until golden. Remove from the oven and let cool completely.

In a microwave-safe bowl, combine the white chocolate chips and ½ cup of the cream and melt in the microwave in 20-second increments, stopping to stir each time, until completely smooth. Set aside to cool.

In a medium-size mixing bowl, using an electric mixer, whip the remaining 2 cups of cream with the powdered sugar until stiff peaks form.

In a separate bowl, whip together the cream cheese, white chocolate mixture, and vanilla and almond extracts. Beat for 2 minutes until completely smooth.

Fold in the sweetened whipped cream by hand.

Spread the white chocolate cream filling into the cooled puff pastry crust. Chill for at least 2 hours to allow the filling to set.

Top with the fresh raspberries just before serving and sprinkle with the grated white chocolate.

VANILLA MIXED FRUIT COMPOTE

This fruit salad consists of both canned and fresh, in-season fruit, making it fitting for most any time of year. It's amazingly simple to make and can be served as a dessert, as a snack, or for breakfast or brunch. Pair it with quiche or a hearty breakfast casserole or serve it as a lighter treat when hosting a special tea party with friends.

Yield: 10 servings

½ cup walnuts or pecans, plus more for serving (optional)
2 small apples, cored and cubed
1 medium-size banana, cut into chunks
2 tablespoons freshly squeezed lemon juice
1 (3.4-ounce) package instant vanilla pudding mix
1 cup pineapple juice
¼ teaspoon pure almond extract
1 fresh pineapple, cored and cubed
1 (15-ounce) can mixed fruit cocktail, drained
1 (15-ounce) can mandarin oranges, drained
1 (8-ounce) jar maraschino cherries, drained and halved
10 vanilla wafers (optional)

Preheat the oven to 350°F. Place the chopped nuts in a single layer on a baking sheet. Toast for 6 to 8 minutes, then set aside to cool completely.

Toss the apple and banana pieces with the lemon juice.

In medium-size mixing bowl, whisk together the pudding mix, pineapple juice, and almond extract for 1 to 2 minutes, or until thickened.

Add all the fruit and the cooled nuts. Mix well.

Chill thoroughly for at least 3 hours prior to serving.

Divide among 10 decorative bowls or parfait glasses and garnish with additional nuts and vanilla wafers prior to serving, if desired.

Store chilled.

BANANA PUDDING PARFAITS

Banana pudding is an obsession and I've never found a variation that I didn't like. Clearly, I'm not alone. Banana pudding is so popular that you're likely to find several versions proudly displayed on the dessert table at any special get-together.

Traditionally, this is a layered dessert very much like a trifle, making it the perfect choice for these easy-to-assemble parfaits. It's the luscious homemade vanilla custard that sets this banana pudding apart, and the parfait glasses make for a spectacular presentation, too.

Yield: 8 (8-ounce) parfaits (see Cook's Note)

1 (12-ounce) can evaporated milk
1 cup granulated sugar
½ cup all-purpose flour
⅛ teaspoon salt
6 large egg yolks
2½ cups half-and-half
2 tablespoons salted butter
1 tablespoon pure vanilla extract
1 (11-ounce) box vanilla wafers
6 medium-size bananas, sliced
1 (8-ounce) container frozen whipped topping, thawed

In a medium-size mixing bowl, whisk together the evaporated milk, sugar, flour, and salt until the sugar has dissolved and no lumps remain. Pour into a heavy-bottomed saucepan and cook over medium-high heat, stirring constantly to prevent sticking, just until warmed.

In the same mixing bowl, whisk together the egg yolks and half-and-half. While whisking, gradually add to the warmed mixture in the saucepan.

Lower the heat to medium and gently cook, stirring, for 10 to 15 minutes, or until thickened.

Remove from the heat and add the butter and vanilla. Mix well. If the custard appears lumpy, press through a fine-mesh sieve to smooth.

Pour the custard into a bowl and press a piece of plastic wrap on top. Allow the custard to cool slightly while you prepare the remaining ingredients.

To assemble, arrange three or four whole vanilla wafers in the bottom of each parfait glass, reserving eight whole vanilla wafers for garnishing. In a separate bowl, crush all the remaining vanilla wafers.

Over the whole vanilla wafers, add a layer of sliced banana (about 4 slices per layer), then cover with about ¼ cup of warm custard. Repeat the layers, beginning with crushed vanilla wafers. Reserving ½ cup of crushed wafers for the top plus 8 whole wafers for garnish, continue layering until all the ingredients have been equally divided among the parfait glasses ending with vanilla custard.

Top each parfait with a dollop of whipped cream. Sprinkle each with the reserved crushed vanilla wafers and garnish with 1 whole wafer.

Chill until serving.

COOK'S NOTE:
Depending on the size of the parfait glasses, the yield may vary slightly.

Traditional Holiday Favorites

The holidays have always been incredibly special for my family, filled with Southern traditions, food, and fun—each event a memory in the making. In particular, I recall how Christmas was celebrated at my grandparents' home. Christmas was Granma Vera's most favorite time of the year. She hosted the family party and planned months beforehand. The kitchen table was abounding with scrumptious holiday savory bites and sweet treats. There were group games to play and prizes to be won by everyone; she made sure we all went home a winner.

Granma Vera was a notorious fan of icicles to decorate her Christmas tree. Such a fan that we weren't always sure whether there was an *actual tree* under the decorations. I recall one year when her tree was so icicle-laden that it collapsed and fell into the middle of the living room floor as if it had just given up. It was too funny to be upsetting even to her. The vision of that Christmas tree lying on the floor remains one of our most favorite holiday memories.

Family Christmas traditions change a bit through the years, as those who hosted are no longer with us. However, we continue to make a special effort to include some of those same activities in our holiday celebration and indulging in some of the same goodies that we shared together. In doing so, it keeps them close to our heart and those precious holiday memories alive forever. Hopefully, minus the toppled Christmas tree.

CHEDDAR BACON PIMIENTO CHEESE BALL

Cheese balls are often thought of as a vintage appetizer. That said, I can't imagine hosting a holiday celebration without one or two on my appetizer table. I thought it would be tasty to combine a traditional cheese ball with another Southern classic: pimiento cheese. The addition of bacon elevates this savory goody into a category all its own. Serve this smoky cheese ball with assorted crackers or bread rounds for a bite-size tidbit to be enjoyed at the holidays or any time of year.

Yield: 16 servings

1 cup chopped pecans

8 ounces cream cheese, softened

2 tablespoons real mayonnaise

1 teaspoon onion powder

½ teaspoon garlic salt

½ teaspoon garlic powder

¼ teaspoon Worcestershire sauce

Pinch of cayenne pepper

1½ cups shredded sharp cheddar cheese

4 tablespoons chopped fresh chives, divided

1 (2-ounce) jar diced pimientos, well drained

8 slices bacon, cooked and crumbled, divided

Preheat the oven to 350°F. Spread the chopped pecans in a single layer on a baking pan. Roast for 6 to 8 minutes, then set aside to cool completely.

In a medium-size mixing bowl, using an electric mixer, whip together the cream cheese, mayonnaise, onion powder, garlic salt, garlic powder, Worcestershire sauce, and pepper.

By hand, fold in the cheddar cheese, 3 tablespoons of the chives, the pimientos, and all but ¼ cup of the crumbled bacon. Shape the cream cheese mixture into a ball.

On a piece of wax paper, mix together the toasted pecans, the remaining tablespoon of the chives, and the reserved ¼ cup of bacon. Roll the cheese ball in the mixture until fully coated.

Wrap tightly in plastic wrap, reshape into a ball, and chill overnight.

Allow the cheese ball to sit at room temperature for 1 hour prior to serving with assorted crackers or cocktail bread rounds.

SEA-SALTED PRALINE PECAN BAKED BRIE

This decadent baked brie is ideal for holiday parties. It's oh-so-simple to make and the rich praline topping pairs beautifully with the creamy warm Brie. Serve it with fruit-laced crispbread, crackers, and fresh apple or pear wedges and it's sure to be a starter that will delight your holiday guests.

Yield: 16 servings

1 (19.6-ounce) wheel Brie cheese
⅔ cup roughly chopped pecans
½ cup packed light brown sugar
¼ cup heavy cream
3 tablespoons salted butter
1 teaspoon pure vanilla extract
½ teaspoon sea salt

Preheat the oven to 350°F. Trim a thin slice from the top of the Brie and discard. Place, cut side up, on a parchment-lined baking sheet. Place the chopped pecans in a single layer on a separate pan. Bake the pecans for 6 to 8 minutes, then remove from the oven and set aside to cool. Bake the Brie for 10 to 15 minutes total, or until the cheese has softened and is beginning to melt.

Meanwhile, in a heavy-bottomed saucepan over medium-high heat, combine the brown sugar, cream, and butter and bring to a boil, stirring constantly, then lower the heat to a simmer and continue to cook for 2 minutes.

Remove from the heat and add the vanilla and pecans. Mix well.

Gently transfer the baked Brie to a serving platter.

Drizzle with the pecan sauce and sprinkle with the sea salt.

Serve immediately with crispbread, crackers, and fresh apple or pear wedges.

CHIVE CREAM CHEESE SAUSAGE BALLS

It wouldn't be a football or holiday party at our house without sausage balls on the menu. Sausage balls are sort of an old-school hors d'oeuvre, which is precisely why I love them. This chive and onion cream cheese version has a splash of brown mustard that expands the flavor palate just enough to give them an update.

Yield: 48 sausage balls

8 ounces chive and onion cream cheese, softened
2 tablespoons spicy brown mustard, plus more for serving
1 teaspoon garlic powder
1 pound breakfast pork sausage
2 cups biscuit baking mix (e.g., Bisquick)
2 cups freshly shredded sharp cheddar cheese

Preheat the oven to 400°F and line two baking sheets with parchment paper. Set aside.

Using an electric mixer, in a medium-size bowl, whip together the cream cheese, mustard, and garlic powder. Add the sausage. Mix on low speed until combined. Add the baking mix 1 cup at a time. Mix until the baking mix is fully incorporated with the sausage.

Use a nonstick spatula to mix in the cheddar cheese by hand.

Roll into 1-inch balls and place 1 inch apart on the prepared baking sheet.

Bake for 22 to 25 minutes, or until golden and cooked through. Serve with additional mustard for dipping.

WHITE CHOCOLATE FROSTED CHERRY COCONUT BARS

These no-bake bars are a spin-off of Granma Vera's famous holiday icebox fruit cake. Christmas was her absolute favorite time of the year. From the decorations to the icicle-laden Christmas tree, the family Christmas parties, gift giving, games, and prizes, she reveled in it all. Her icebox fruit cake could be found nestled next to the world's greatest boiled custard in her fridge every holiday season.

Yield: 24 pieces or 48 triangles

1 (14-ounce) sweetened shredded coconut, divided

1 cup chopped walnuts

1 (16-ounce) bag mini marshmallows

1 (14.5-ounce) can sweetened condensed milk

2 tablespoons salted butter

1 (16-ounce) candied cherries, chopped

1 teaspoon pure almond extract

4 cups graham cracker crumbs

1 (12-ounce) package white chocolate chips

½ cup heavy cream

Line a 9 × 13-inch baking pan with wax paper, leaving enough overhang to easily lift out the bars for cutting. Set aside.

Preheat the oven to 350°F. Spread ½ cup of the coconut and all the walnuts separately on a baking sheet. Toast for 8 minutes, or until golden, stirring halfway through. Remove from the oven and set aside to cool, reserving the toasted coconut for topping.

In a medium-size, heavy-bottomed saucepan, melt together the marshmallows, sweetened condensed milk, and butter. Cook over medium heat, stirring constantly to prevent sticking. After the marshmallows have melted, add the cherries and almond extract. Remove from the heat.

Working quickly, mix the graham cracker crumbs, remaining untoasted coconut, and the toasted walnuts into the melted marshmallow mixture. Stir until fully moistened. Press firmly and evenly into the waxed paper–lined pan.

In microwave-safe bowl, combine the white chocolate chips and cream and melt in 20-second increments, stopping to stir each time, until completely smooth. Pour over the cake batter and sprinkle with the reserved ½ cup of toasted coconut.

Chill overnight. Cut into squares or into triangles. Store chilled.

CUTOUT CREAM CHEESE SUGAR COOKIES

During the Christmas season, this is the recipe I use when we bake cookies for Santa. The cream cheese and butter combine to give a flaky, melt-in-your-mouth texture. For the best results, the dough should be made in advance and chilled until firm before attempting to roll. Make sure you start on a floured surface and flour the rolling pin, too, and then you're set to begin the cookie cutter fun. Keep any unused dough chilled between batches so it will remain firm.

I've included a glaze recipe that dries shiny but maintains a soft texture, making it the perfect topping for these holiday goodies. I have it on good authority that this cookie is one of Santa's absolute favorites and that after dropping off gifts, he leaves nothing behind on the plate but the crumbs.

Yield: 24 cookies (yield may vary, depending on size of cutters)

Cookies:

3 cups all-purpose flour, plus more for dusting

½ teaspoon salt

¼ teaspoon ground nutmeg

1 cup (2 sticks, or 8 ounces) salted butter, at room temperature

4 ounces cream cheese, softened

2 teaspoons pure vanilla extract

½ teaspoon pure almond extract

2 large egg yolks

To make the cookies: Sift together the flour, salt, and nutmeg. Set aside.

In the bowl of a stand mixer, cream together the butter, cream cheese, and vanilla and almond extracts. Beat for 2 minutes, or until fluffy and light.

Add the egg yolks, one at a time, beating well after each addition, then beat for 2 minutes on high speed. The creamed mixture should be fluffy and light yellow in color.

Gradually add the flour mixture, mixing on low speed until combined. Divide the dough in half and shape each portion into a disk. Wrap in plastic wrap and chill for 2 hours, or until firm.

To bake, preheat the oven to 375°F. Line two cookie sheets with parchment paper. Set aside.

On a floured surface, roll one disk of the chilled dough to ⅓-inch thickness. Cut into your desired shapes, using cookie cutters dipped in flour. Place the cookies at least 1½ inches apart on prepared cookie sheets.

Bake for 10 to 12 minutes, or until the edges are golden. Remove from the oven and let cool completely on a cooling rack before glazing or decorating.

Glaze:

1 cup powdered sugar

2 tablespoons light corn syrup

¼ teaspoon pure almond extract

¼ teaspoon clear butter flavoring or
pure vanilla extract

1 to 3 teaspoons water

Gel food coloring

Sprinkles or seasonal nonpareils, for
decorating

To make the glaze: In a small mixing bowl, stir together the powdered sugar, corn syrup, almond extract, and butter flavoring or vanilla. Add water 1 teaspoon at a time, repeating until the glaze reaches spreading consistency, then color as desired.

Frost the baked cookies and decorate with sprinkles or seasonal nonpareils. Lay in a single layer to dry.

The glazed cookies may be stored at room temperature. Do not stack.

COOK'S NOTE:

These cookies may also be made as a drop cookie prior to chilling, if desired.

CHRISTMAS EVE DATE NUT COOKIES

These powdered sugar-coated date nut cookies have been a holiday family tradition for as long as I can remember. They bake crisp yet delicate on the inside, with an element of chewiness from the chopped dates tucked away inside the dough. The dates make them so appetizing and the toasted pecans give them Southern flair.

Yield: About 2 dozen cookies

1 cup (2 sticks, or 8 ounces) salted
    butter, at room temperature
2½ cups powdered sugar, divided
1 teaspoon pure vanilla extract
2 cups self-rising flour
1 cup chopped dates
½ cup finely chopped pecans

Preheat the oven to 350°F. Line a cookie sheet with parchment paper. Set aside.

In a medium-size mixing bowl, using an electric mixer, cream together the butter, ½ cup of the powdered sugar, and the vanilla. Beat for 2 minutes, or until light yellow and fluffy. Reduce the speed of the mixer and add the flour, beating just until combined.

Stir in the dates and pecans by hand.

Roll into balls or logs or shape into crescents and place on the prepared cookie sheet.

Bake for 12 to 16 minutes, or until firm but not browned. Meanwhile place the remaining 2 cups of powdered sugar in a shallow bowl.

Remove the cookies from the oven, immediately roll them in powdered sugar, and place on a cooling rack to cool completely.

Store tightly covered.

TURTLE CARAMEL-DIPPED APPLES

When the cool breezes of fall begin to blow and apples are in season, it's time to enjoy this classic caramel treat. When you combine brown sugar and butter, the end result could only be good, so skip the wrapped caramels and make homemade caramel for dipping apples instead. To make turtle-coated apples, dip Granny Smith apples in gooey homemade caramel, then roll in mini chocolate chips and toasted pecans. After drying, wrap them in cellophane and tie each with a pretty ribbon, turning them into a homemade party favor for kids, teachers, and beyond. Alternatively, it's also acceptable if you'd like to eat them yourself.

Yield: 10 dipped apples

1 to 2 cups chopped pecans
10 medium-size Granny Smith apples
¾ cup (1½ sticks, or 6 ounces) salted butter
2 cups packed light brown sugar
¾ cup light corn syrup
¼ cup dark corn syrup
¼ teaspoon salt
1 (14-ounce) can sweetened condensed milk
2 teaspoons pure vanilla extract
1 to 2 cups mini chocolate chips

Preheat the oven to 350°F. Spread the pecans in a single layer on a baking sheet. Toast for 6 to 8 minutes, then set aside and let cool completely.

Wash and dry the apples thoroughly. Remove the stem and insert a food-safe stick into the center. Set aside.

In a medium-size, heavy-bottomed saucepan over medium heat, melt together the butter, brown sugar, light and dark corn syrup, and salt, stirring constantly to prevent sticking.

Add the sweetened condensed milk. Gently bring to a boil, stirring constantly. Lower the heat and cook until a candy thermometer reaches 225°F. This may take 15 to 20 minutes.

Remove from the heat and mix in the vanilla.

Dip each apple into the caramel, turning evenly to coat. Immediately dip into the chopped pecans and mini chocolate chips.

Place onto a wax paper-lined baking sheet. Chill until set.

Bring to room temperature to allow the caramel to soften prior to serving. Store chilled.

CHOCOLATE PEANUT BUTTER SWIRL FUDGE

What would the holidays be without fudge as part of the rich, handmade confections? This fudge combines my boys' two favorite flavors; chocolate and peanut butter. The recipe yields a large batch, making it perfect for homemade gift-giving, too. There's plenty to share with the special people in your life and some to keep for yourself to enjoy.

Yield: 150 (1-inch) squares

4 tablespoons salted butter, plus more for pan

4 cups granulated sugar

1½ cups half-and-half

½ teaspoon salt

⅓ cup smooth peanut butter

1¼ cups (7 ounces) marshmallow fluff

1 teaspoon pure vanilla extract

4 cups semisweet chocolate chips

1 (12-ounce) package peanut butter baking chips

2 cups dry-roasted peanuts, roughly chopped

Line a jelly-roll pan with heavy-duty aluminum foil. Butter liberally. Set aside.

In a large pot over high heat, melt together the sugar, half-and-half, butter, and salt. Bring to a boil, stirring constantly, then lower the heat to medium and allow to boil for 7 minutes, continuing to stir.

Meanwhile, in a small, microwave-safe mixing bowl, heat the peanut butter for 20 seconds to melt. Remove from the microwave and add ¼ cup of the marshmallow fluff, mixing until fully combined. Set aside.

After 7 minutes, add the vanilla, chocolate chips, and peanut butter chips to the boiling sugar mixture. Remove from the heat. Stir until the chips have completely melted, then add the remaining marshmallow fluff and chopped peanuts. Mix until fully combined.

Working quickly, spread into the prepared pan. Dollop the peanut butter mixture over the chocolate mixture. Use a knife to swirl through the fudge.

Let cool completely at room temperature or chill for faster setup. Cut into 1-inch squares.

SALTINE TOFFEE CRUNCH

This sweet and salty cracker candy is addicting. It starts with saltine crackers that are topped with a buttery caramel sauce and then finishes with milk chocolate. After breaking into pieces it can be packaged in goodie bags to be shared as a gift. Plan on making a batch just for munching as it tends to mysteriously disappear with no trace left behind.

Yield: About 1½ pounds

2 to 3 sleeves saltine crackers
2 cups granulated sugar
1 cup (2 sticks, or 8 ounces) salted butter
2 teaspoons pure vanilla extract
1 (11-ounce) package milk chocolate chips
1 cup English toffee bits

Preheat the oven to 350°F. Line a standard 17 × 12-inch rimmed baking sheet with parchment paper. Arrange the saltine crackers side by side in the pan in a single layer, touching but not overlapping. Set aside.

In a small saucepan over medium-high heat, melt together the sugar and butter. Cook, stirring constantly, until the sugar has dissolved and is no longer grainy.

Remove from the heat and add the vanilla. Mix well. Pour evenly over the crackers

Bake for 12 minutes. Remove from the oven and allow the bubbles to die down.

Sprinkle the milk chocolate chips over the hot toffee. Wait 5 minutes.

Spread the melted chocolate over the toffee and sprinkle evenly with the toffee bits. Refrigerate for 1 hour, or until set, then break or cut into pieces.

SLOW COOKER CHOCOLATE CANDY BAR CRUNCH

Slow cooker candy is a delightful holiday tradition. The biggest advantage to using a slow cooker is that it does the task of gently melting the chocolate for you. The crushed Butterfinger candy bars are then added to the warm peanuts and melted chocolate at the end of slow cooking. To make the candy, drop clusters into festive cupcake liners or dollop onto wax paper. After the clusters dry, it's time to devour.

Yield: 48 large or 96 mini candies (yield may vary)

1 (16-ounce) container unsalted dry roasted peanuts

1 (10-ounce) container cocktail peanuts

1 (12-ounce) package semisweet chocolate chips

1 (4-ounce) package German chocolate, chopped

24 ounces chocolate almond bark, roughly chopped

24 ounces vanilla almond bark, roughly chopped

4 full-size Butterfinger candy bars, crushed

In an oval 6-quart slow cooker, layer the peanuts, semisweet chocolate chips, German chocolate, chocolate almond bark, and vanilla almond bark.

Cover and cook on LOW for 3 hours. Uncover and stir.

Mix in the crushed Butterfinger candy bars, reserving ½ cup for garnish.

Line the cups of four 12-cup standard muffin tins with decorative liners. Use a 2-ounce ice-cream scoop or tablespoon to drop chocolate clusters into the liners. Sprinkle the tops with the Butterfinger crumbs while the chocolate is wet.

Allow to cool and set.

BAKING SUBSTITUTIONS

It never fails; you begin a baking project only to discover you're missing a key ingredient. To achieve the best results when making any recipe, you should follow the recipe as written with little to no substitutions. However, if you find yourself in a bind, this is a great reference tool.

Keep in mind, when substituting ingredients, it may also be necessary to make adjustments to other components as well. One example would be the need to adjust the amount of liquid called for in the recipe if using a substitute that adds liquid. This list is a compilation of the most common baking substitutions.

Eggs: Per whole egg, use:
- ¼ cup liquid egg substitute
- 2½ tablespoons powdered egg substitute plus 2½ tablespoons water
- ¼ cup puréed silken tofu
- ½ mashed banana plus ½ teaspoon baking powder
- 3 tablespoons mayonnaise

Salted Butter: Per 1 cup (for unsalted butter—omit salt), use:
- 1 cup shortening plus ½ teaspoon salt
- 1 cup margarine plus ½ teaspoon salt
- ⅞ cup vegetable oil plus ½ teaspoon salt

Fats for baking: Per 1 cup, use:
- 1 cup applesauce
- 1 cup fruit purée

Shortening: Use same amount of butter.

Sour cream: Use same amount of plain yogurt.

Buttermilk: Per 1 cup, use:
- 1 cup whole milk plus 1 tablespoon freshly squeezed lemon juice or white vinegar. Let sit for 5 minutes.
- 1 cup plain yogurt

Evaporated milk: Per 1 cup, use 1 cup light cream.

Heavy cream: Per 1 cup, use 1 cup evaporated milk (for baking only; evaporated milk *will not* whip like whipping cream).

Half-and-half: Per 1 cup, use ½ cup whole milk plus ½ cup heavy cream.

Cream cheese: Per 1 cup, use:
- 1 cup pureed cottage cheese
- 1 cup plain yogurt
- 1 cup mascarpone cheese

Lemon juice: Use same amount of vinegar, freshly squeezed lime juice, or white wine.

Vinegar: Use same amount of freshly squeezed lemon juice.

Corn syrup: Per 1 cup, use:
- 1 cup honey
- 1¼ cups granulated sugar plus ⅓ cup water (mix until dissolved)

Brown sugar: Per 1 cup use:
- 1 cup granulated sugar plus ¼ cup molasses and decrease liquid in recipe by ¼ cup
- 1 cup granulated sugar
- 1¼ cups powdered sugar

Cake flour: Per 1 cup, use 1 cup all-purpose flour minus 2 tablespoons; replace with 2 tablespoons cornstarch.

Self-rising flour: Per 1 cup, use 1 cup all-purpose flour plus 1½ teaspoons baking powder and ½ teaspoon salt.

Baking powder: Per 1 teaspoon, use ¼ teaspoon baking soda plus ½ teaspoon cream of tartar.

Cream of tartar: Per 1 teaspoon, use 2 teaspoons freshly squeezed lemon juice or vinegar.

Unsweetened cocoa powder: Per 1 ounce use 1 (1-ounce) square unsweetened chocolate

Unsweetened chocolate: Per 1 ounce, use 3 tablespoons unsweetened cocoa powder plus 1 tablespoon shortening or vegetable oil.

Semisweet chocolate: Per 1 ounce, use:
- 1 (1-ounce) square unsweetened chocolate plus 4 teaspoons granulated sugar
- 1 ounce semisweet chocolate chips plus 1 teaspoon shortening

Allspice: Per 1 teaspoon, use ½ teaspoon ground cinnamon, ¼ teaspoon ground ginger, and ¼ teaspoon ground cloves

DIY pumpkin pie spice: Makes about ¼ cup:
2 tablespoons ground cinnamon
1 tablespoon ground ginger
1 teaspoon ground cloves
1 teaspoon ground nutmeg
1 teaspoon ground allspice
¼ teaspoon ground cardamom

DIY apple pie spice: Makes about ¼ cup:
2 tablespoons ground cinnamon
2 teaspoons ground nutmeg
1 teaspoon ground ginger
½ teaspoon ground allspice or cloves
½ teaspoon ground cardamom

CLOSING THOUGHTS

When I think of mealtime, it's much more than an opportunity to feed hungry mouths. It's the one moment of the day that you can pause and give thanks, count your blessings, and enjoy a time of chatter with the ones in your life who mean the most. It's not about the quantity of dishes that you serve, but the quality of the time spent together. I'm a firm believer that cooking is an outward expression of love. You can show that love by making a meal filled with homemade comfort to lift spirits after a hectic day. It's up to each of us to make the absolute most of those precious moments spent around the kitchen table. Always keep in mind that the events of today are shaping tomorrow's memories. Make them the very best.

ACKNOWLEDGMENTS

First, I'd like to thank God for the opportunities that He has given to me and for guiding my path along life's journey. To my mom, Barbara, and her mother, Granma Vera. To my paternal Granma Minnie, Great-Aunt Beulah, and mother-in-law, Thelma. Through the years they've all shown me what it is to be a Southern lady and each of them has instilled in me her way of cooking, how to prepare the foods we love, and how to serve them with grace, charm, and style. To my own family, who continue to inspire me every single day and for being my official taste testers. I can't thank my husband and sweet boys enough for their willingness to eat pumpkin pie in August and Valentine's Day candy at Christmas. My incredibly creative sons who sit and design art at our kitchen counter telling me funny stories about their day while I mix up my next winning recipe. They are the ultimate inspiration.

Lastly, a heartfelt thanks to the editorial team at The Countryman Press for believing in me and turning my passion for cooking and baking into this beautiful book. I will be forever grateful.

INDEX

Boldface page numbers indicate illustrations.